BILLY GRAHAM
Evangelistic Assc
Always Good N

D0206706

Dear Friend,

I am pleased to send you this copy of *Reborn* by Clayton King, a pastor at NewSpring Church in Anderson, S.C. His Bible teaching has been heard on our radio station, The LightFM, for the last decade.

God's Word tells us that no matter how hard we try, we can't fix ourselves. Our only hope is a relationship with His Son, and He promises that "*if anyone is in Christ, he is a new creation; old things have passed away; behold, all things have become new*" (2 Corinthians 5:17, NKJV). In *Reborn*, Clayton invites you to discover the Scriptural accounts of 12 broken people whose lives were radically changed when they came face-to-face with Jesus Christ. This powerful book also features the stories of modern men and women who have struggled with addiction, greed, and depression—and found healing in Christ. It's my prayer that *Reborn* will help you draw closer to God and spend transforming time in His Word.

For more than 70 years, God has used the Billy Graham Evangelistic Association (BGEA) and friends like you to reach people all over the world with the Gospel. I'm so thankful for the ways He has worked—and for what He is continuing to do in the lives of men, women, and children today.

If you represent one of the lives the Lord has touched, we would love to hear from you. Your story has the power to impact the lives of so many others. May God richly bless you.

Sincerely,

Franklin Graham
President

If you would like to know more about our ministry, please contact us:

IN THE U.S.:
Billy Graham Evangelistic Association
1 Billy Graham Parkway
Charlotte, NC 28201-0001
BillyGraham.org
info@bgea.org
Toll-free: 1-877-247-2426

IN CANADA:
Billy Graham Evangelistic
    Association of Canada
20 Hopewell Way NE
Calgary, AB T3J 5H5
BillyGraham.ca
Toll-free: 1-888-393-0003

"Whenever Clayton King talks, whether on stage or off stage, it leads to Jesus. This book is full of stories—both biblical and firsthand—about what it looks like when people meet Jesus. It's inspiring and challenging to be reminded of those encounters. This book will inspire and challenge you too."

Mack Brock, worship leader and songwriter

"For the more than two decades I've preached the gospel with Clayton, I've never known anyone better at opening up the life of Jesus and the struggles of the human heart and showing how these two were made for each other. *Reborn* is Clayton at his best."

J. D. Greear, PhD, pastor of The Summit Church, Raleigh-Durham

"*Reborn* embarks you on a journey that awakens your purpose by following trails filled with wonderful stories and eye-opening truths. Clayton King's encounter with Jesus didn't simply change him but inspired him to share what he found in hopes that it would change you as well!"

Joseph Sojourner, pastor of The Studio Gathering and creative director of Two Cents Creative Thinkers

"*Reborn* proves that a book can be theologically deep, culturally rich, and spiritually uplifting. It's a simple and yet profound look into the person of Jesus Christ as revealed in his interactions with notorious sinners, elite professionals, marginalized outcasts, and fantastic failures. You will be spellbound by this book."

Santiago "Jimmy" Mellado, president and CEO of Compassion International

"*Reborn* is gospel-focused and theologically deep while remaining practically simple. You'll laugh, you'll cry, you'll be encouraged, and you'll be challenged. Thank you, Clayton, for always reminding us of what matters most."

Michelle Myers, founder of she works HIS way

"This book is so powerful—it points you to the gospel that can change everything in your life for the better. My friend Clayton King has one primary message in his life, and you can sense his heart beating in the middle of these words for this One thing that changes everything."

Matt Brown, evangelist, author of *Truth Plus Love*, and founder of Think Eternity

"Clayton King is the most captivating evangelist of our day, and *Reborn* is his most riveting treatment of the gospel yet. A natural-born storyteller, he draws upon stories from the Bible and everyday life to reveal the gospel's explosive power to transform lives. Buy a copy for yourself and dozen for your friends."

Bruce Riley Ashford, author of *The Gospel of Our King*
and *Letters to an American Christian*

"Clayton's passion for people is only matched by his passion for Jesus. This book is about these two passions—passions that invite us to rethink ours. Thank you, Clayton, for writing this book and for challenging us."

Naeem Fazal, pastor of Mosaic Church
and author of *Ex-Muslim*

"In *Reborn*, Clayton combines his compelling storytelling ability with rich historical context that sheds refreshing light on New Testament characters. *Reborn* will make you both laugh and cry, but mostly it will show you again how beautiful Jesus really is."

Bruce Frank, lead pastor of Biltmore Church

"As believers, we are called to a higher standard of treating people. Everyone. Everyone has value because God gave them value. My longtime friend and incredible leader Clayton King is diving into this conversation because it matters, and Clayton lives out this message!"

Tyler Reagin, author of *Life-Giving Leader*

"*Reborn* illuminates the full beauty of Jesus and makes you want to share the gospel like you've just experienced it for the first time! In his spectacular Clayton style, the book is brilliant, funny, and deeply emotional. You'll laugh, cry, and ultimately fall in love with Jesus on another level!"

Chuck Balsamo, extraordinary life expert, pastor of
Destiny Family Center, speaker, and coach

"Clayton King clearly and authentically unpacks the incredible power of the gospel and the hope found in Jesus. His stories, passion, and insight will give you fresh perspective. It's classic Clayton style—real, funny, and straight to the gut! Jesus is the greatest leader ever, and *Reborn* illustrates the personal influence with which Jesus changed the world."

Brad Lomenick, author of *The Catalyst Leader* and *H3
Leadership* and former president of Catalyst

"Many desire change but believe it just isn't possible. In *Reborn*, Clayton King shows that the same power of Jesus to change lives in the Bible is presently at work among us. When we encounter Christ, our lives are transformed. Broken people—like you and me—will find hope in the pages of this book."

Christopher Yuan, DMin, speaker and author of *Out of a Far Country* and *Holy Sexuality and the Gospel*

"The message of *Reborn* is a message everyone needs to hear or hear again. Clayton is a masterful storyteller. He has a way of capturing your imagination and your heart as he connects stories in the Scriptures to stories still unfolding today. He shines light on the reality that Jesus truly does change everything."

Daniel Floyd, senior pastor of Lifepoint Church

"I've always been inspired by Clayton's passion for Jesus. It's contagious and pure and real. Through *Reborn*, you'll get a front-row seat to this. This book will encourage your faith and open your eyes to the abundance that is in that one Name. It reminds you that hope is here. Some moments can change everything."

Carson Case, speaker, pastor, and author of *Born For It*

"I was nineteen years old when I first heard Clayton preach the message of what it means to be reborn. Picking up this book years later, I am reminded all over again of the power of the proclamation of the simple gospel. As Clayton writes, 'Jesus extended hope and salvation to real people who desperately needed it.' And one of my favorite things to be able to say about my friend is that he is so much like his Savior that way."

Meredith Knox, training director of Central Fuse and worship leader of NewSpring Church

"Jesus was about people, and *Reborn* paints a clear picture of just how Jesus treated those he came in contact with. The more I read, the more I was inspired."

Brad Cooper, lead pastor of direction and culture, NewSpring Church

"*Reborn* is captivating! What Jesus came to do—seek and save—is put on full display. After reading story after story, encounter after encounter of how people were saved, changed, and reborn, I am ready to charge hell with a bucket of water and a half-loaded water gun! This book will cause every reader to be moved to action. The nonbeliever will meet Jesus instantly. The believer will seek the lost urgently. I. Am. Ready."

James D. Noble, PhD, vice president of diversity and inclusion, Anderson University.

"*Reborn* is a beautiful story woven of powerful testimonies from all around the world. Clayton shares how Jesus has radically changed individuals from the inside out from every nation, and this book was such encouragement for me personally. It's full of hope while telling the full truth of the gospel. I am so thankful it exists!"

Chelsea Hurst, author of *Your Own Beautiful* and *Above All Else*

"Clayton's insight takes you deeper into the narrative of the gospel message and portrays Jesus clearly and accurately. As someone who's preached from the Gospels for years, I saw things I'd never seen before as Jesus is painted in a fresh perspective as both a Jewish rabbi and the Son of God. It's a profound look into the Person of Jesus Christ as revealed in his interactions with notorious sinners, elite professionals, marginalized outcasts, and fantastic failures."

Nick Hurst, preacher, evangelist, and husband to Chelsea Hurst

"A book for *all* people. *Reborn* will captivate the reader with its funny, tearful, deep, and unveiling ride from rich history to modern-day stories about the transformation from death to life through the gospel and love of Jesus Christ."

Joby Martin, lead pastor of The Church of Eleven22, Jacksonville, Florida

"We all have decisions to make *every day*, and each decision renders some kind of consequence. If you decide to see Clayton preach, the consequence could be that you'll be moved emotionally or you might learn something, but for sure you'll be entertained. If you decide to truly meet Jesus, *everything* will change. *Reborn* is a wonderful book about people who made life-changing decisions."

Jeff Jarrett, world heavyweight champion, WWE and WCW

REBORN

How Encountering Jesus Changes Everything

CLAYTON KING

BakerBooks
a division of Baker Publishing Group
www.BakerBooks.com

This *Billy Graham Library Selection* special edition is published
with permission from Baker Books.

©2020 by Clayton King

Published by Baker Books
a division of Baker Publishing Group
P.O. Box 6287, Grand Rapids, MI 49516-6287
www.bakerbooks.com

Printed in the United States of America

Library of Congress Cataloging-in-Publication Data
Names: King, Clayton, 1972– author.
Title: Reborn : how encountering Jesus changes everything / Clayton King.
Description: Grand Rapids, Michigan : Baker Books, a division of Baker Publishing Group, 2020.
Identifiers: LCCN 2019047381 | ISBN 9780801019609 (paperback) | ISBN 9781593286699 (BGEA Edition)
Subjects: LCSH: Conversion—Biblical teaching. | Christian converts—Biography.
Classification: LCC BV4932 .K56 2020 | DDC 248.4—dc23
LC record available at https://lccn.loc.gov/2019047381

In keeping with biblical principles of creation stewardship, Baker Publishing Group advocates the responsible use of our natural resources. As a member of the Green Press Initiative, our company uses recycled paper when possible. The text paper of this book is composed in part of post-consumer waste.

20 21 22 23 24 25 26   7 6 5 4 3 2 1

Reborn is dedicated to my spiritual fathers
who taught me to love Scripture,
to love Jesus, and to love the gospel.

Joe King

Wilkes Skinner

Jake Thornhill

Ronnie Powell

Robert Canoy

Todd Still

Billy Graham

Regi Campbell

David Chadwick

Ricky Mason

Dan Brock

Contents

Foreword by Dr. Derwin L. Gray   11

Introduction: What You Need for a New
   Beginning   15

1. Turn On the Light in Your Life   21
2. What to Do When You Don't Belong   37
3. When You Have Little to Offer   53
4. What to Do When You've Blown It   67
5. Reverse the Curse in Your Life   83
6. Reaching Out to Jesus   99
7. A Heart's Humble Prayer   113
8. Wasted Opportunity   127
9. So You Would Believe   141
10. The Benefit of Doubt   159
11. How Resistance Reveals Jesus   175
12. How Jesus Brings Joy   191
13. How Jesus Restores Relationships   205

Acknowledgments   211

Foreword

Clayton King has been one of my best friends for over twenty years. He's one of the primary reasons I'm a pastor. In 1999, I was freshly retired from the National Football League and not sure what I was supposed to do with my life. Somehow, in a way that only God in his love could orchestrate, I was invited to share my testimony at an evangelistic event Clayton put on in a small North Carolina town. We connected instantly. We've been friends ever since. I suspect that most of my early speaking engagements were because of him. He leveraged his good name on my behalf. Because people trusted him, they trusted me. I will always be grateful to him.

In 2004, when my wife was diagnosed with cancer and had to take time away from our ministry to heal, Clayton and his ministry team took over all of the ministry logistics my wife could no longer handle until she got better. That's the kind of man he is. Clayton is a great preacher, but he's a better man. He loves Jesus, the gospel, and seeing people come to know and love Jesus.

I offer this background information to you as a gift. A book is only as good as the character of the person writing it. Not only does Clayton embody the character of Jesus but he unveils Jesus in his writing. In the pages of *Reborn*, like a tour guide on some great adventure, Clayton is going to lead you to the heart of Jesus. Whether you are exploring who Jesus is or have journeyed with Jesus for a long time, this book is going to transform you.

Clayton has a unique gift of writing. As you read, you will find yourself seeing, tasting, and experiencing the historical, biblical insights he is going to share with you. He has first-hand knowledge of Israel, rooted in his nine trips to the Holy Land. This book paints pictures of beauty and grace that are just captivating. Clayton writes, "To be reborn means to be born of God. As in God gives us a new life. A fresh start. A new identity."

As you read *Reborn*, your hunger for God is going to increase. You are going to want to know him more, and from knowing him more you will find yourself lost in his beauty. You will experience a rebirth and new passion for Jesus. You will find yourself grasping what it means to be "born of God." Literally, God shares his unending, transformative life with you. You become a participant in the very life of God the Father, the Son, and the Holy Spirit. As Paul the apostle writes, "For you died, and your life is now hidden with Christ in God" (Col. 3:3). Along with sharing the life of Jesus, God graciously gives us a new identity. This identity is unchanging because it is rooted in the unchanging redemptive work of Jesus.

In Christ, you are

forever forgiven
as righteous as Jesus
holy and blameless
a beloved child of God

God's dwelling place
God's church
more than a conqueror

I could go on and on. But now it's time for you to read
Reborn.

Dr. Derwin L. Gray, lead pastor of Transformation Church
and author of *The Good Life: What Jesus Teaches
about Happiness* (June 2020, B&H)

Introduction

What You Need for a New Beginning

It was late May in Jerusalem and it was hot, especially where we were standing at 4:00 p.m. on old Mount Zion. The streets were filled with people, both inside the walls of the old city and outside the walls in the new city, and bustling with tour buses and Palestinian and Israeli families heading home for the evening.

Earlier that day, we had gathered in the garden of Gethsemane to read the story of Jesus and his last night with the disciples before he was arrested, tried, and crucified. In the garden, the olive trees are the great-grandchildren of the very olive trees Jesus would have knelt and prayed under two thousand years earlier, descendants from the "olive shoots" that grow from the base of old olive tree matriarchs, mother trees that have given birth to countless thousands of olives throughout the centuries.

That morning we stood where Jesus asked his Father to take away the cup of suffering that awaited him on the cross, and we laid our hands on members of our team who were sick, asking our Father to let the cup of sickness pass by them. The presence of the Spirit was tangible.

Now, nearly eight hours later, on the western side of the Kidron Valley, my friend David Lewkowicz and I stood on a hot sidewalk that felt like an oven baking cookies, looking across to the Mount of Olives and Gethsemane below. In Gethsemane Jesus chose to go through with his mission. All the way. To the cross.

As my friend David and I waited for our bus to pick us up, along with seventy other sweaty American pilgrims, I remembered that fifty yards from where we stood, on the same road, was the grave of Oskar Schindler. As a member of the Nazi party in Germany leading up to WWII, Schindler saved more than 1,200 Jews during the Holocaust by hiring them to work in his factories under the guise of building munitions for Hitler's army.

I mentioned this to David, assuming he'd seen the movie *Schindler's List*. He said, "Are you serious? You know Schindler saved three of my Jewish relatives from the gas chambers, right?"

No. As a matter of fact, I did not know that.

A pastor of an evangelical church in North Carolina, David had wanted to visit the land of his ancestors, and as a Jewish person who believes Jesus is the Messiah, he wanted to walk where Jesus walked. We've been friends for years, but it was in this moment, standing on that hot sidewalk with the old city above us and Gethsemane across from us, that I realized just how practically powerful salvation is.

David was standing less than a football field away from the grave of the man who'd saved his ancestors from certain death in 1944. He'd had no idea he was so close to the source of his family's salvation.

In that moment *salvation* felt more real, more meaningful than it had before. As a pastor, I talk about salvation all the time. It's my job and my calling. And yet, standing there, I felt the weight of salvation in a new way. It was the difference between life and death for David's family. It was the difference between freedom and a concentration camp.

While we're not in danger of being loaded onto a train by Nazis and sent to our death, we're all in danger of being ruined by some sin that seeks to control us. The problems we face are just as deadly and just as eternal.

There is an enemy that seeks to break us and destroy our lives.

The solution is encountering Jesus.

In John 10:10, Jesus clearly states his sole purpose in coming to earth: "The thief comes only to steal and kill and destroy; I have come that they may have life, and have it to the full." That's what this book is about.

The next day we visited two places in Jerusalem where tradition tells us Jesus's tomb is located: the Garden Tomb and the Church of the Holy Sepulchre. Though history and tradition favor the Holy Sepulchre as the most likely location of the empty tomb, the only thing that makes the tomb of Jesus important is that *it's empty*.

> *There is an enemy that seeks to break us and destroy our lives. The solution is encountering Jesus.*

Actually, the only thing that makes Jesus important, if you really want to get down to business, is that his grave has been vacated.

The death of Jesus on the cross secures the forgiveness we need for the sins we have committed. The resurrection of Jesus from the dead opens up for us a new beginning, another chance at life.

The chance to be *reborn*.

What about You?

What would our lives look like if we had a gigantic do-over? If we had the power to change the things in our lives that often seem impossible, wouldn't we do it? Well, we can. By opening our lives up to Jesus, we're inviting true, lasting change that not only makes us better people but also gives us the ability to help others find that same kind of power to change. We can help save others by pointing them to the only source of salvation.

So, what about you? Where are you on your journey? What things in your life need to be changed? Do you need faith to replace your fear? Do you need to know that you're unconditionally loved by God despite your mistakes? Are you searching for deeper meaning in your life beyond school or your job?

You could be a college student struggling with direction, a mom with small kids searching for your purpose, or a successful business owner with a secret addiction that controls you. Maybe you've come to the end of your rope, or you're all out of ideas and your energy is tapped out. Or you just cannot seem to forgive that person who hurt you so deeply. It doesn't matter to Jesus. He sees you. He loves you. He can change you. He's offering you a chance to be reborn.

For almost thirty-five years, I've seen people from all over the planet encounter the person of Jesus in strange, unexpected ways, and I'm more convinced than ever that Jesus does really, truly, literally change everything.

When I began working on the concept for this book, I made a list of all the characters in the New Testament who had some kind of encounter with Jesus I considered profound or fascinating. I wanted to show how Jesus changed everything then and how he still changes people now.

This book will, in part, relive some moments when people I've met were reborn because of an encounter with Jesus. It will also connect these stories with actual women and men in the Bible who had similar experiences when they met Jesus.

Though thousands of years have passed since Jesus walked the earth, people haven't really changed in their basic nature, and Jesus hasn't changed at all. People are still searching, imperfect, and broken, and Jesus is still seeking and saving the lost. He's still giving people a chance at a new life, a do-over, an opportunity to be reborn.

People are still searching, imperfect, and broken, and Jesus is still seeking and saving the lost. He's still giving people a chance at a new life, a do-over, an opportunity to be reborn.

Let me ask you a question: Do you feel like you're walking in the dark sometimes?

Maybe you've spent more time warming a church pew than a barstool and can name the books of the Bible forward and backward, but you've never been reborn by faith in Jesus.

Or perhaps the reverse is true, and you're carrying around the heavy baggage of your past sins and shame. Maybe you're trying to manage your image on the outside, but there's a void on the inside no one can feel but you.

Maybe you've been hurt by the people in your life or even the church, and you're wondering if Jesus is any different. Can you really trust him to help you and not hurt you?

Or maybe you're gripped by anxiety, crushed by heartbreak, consumed by depression, or crippled by fear of what you can't control. The solution to your problem can't be found in a prescription or a pill. You need a Person.

It's not an exaggeration to say that *encountering Jesus changes everything*. Let's take the journey together, through these pages, and see how Jesus has extended hope and salvation to real people who desperately needed it.

As we do, you'll see how he offers salvation to you as well.

ONE

Turn On the Light in Your Life

In his classic book *Eternity in Their Hearts*, Don Richardson chronicles stories of people all over the world, from different cultures and backgrounds, separated by decades and thousands of miles, and the jaw-dropping ways they came to faith in Christ. The book made a profound impression on me as an evangelist, in part because so many of the stories he shares bear striking similarities to people I've known who've been reborn by the unpredictable and unstoppable love of Jesus.

As Richardson cataloged in his book, and missionaries and pastors are increasingly reporting, people by the scores are being introduced to Jesus by . . . well . . . Jesus. From the Himalayas of Nepal to the sand dunes of Saudi Arabia, women and men are reporting meeting Jesus for the first time in visions and dreams. Sometimes he appears to them in broad daylight and tells them that he died on the cross and rose from the dead to save them. Other times he comes to them in their sleep, smiling, with his arms open, inviting them to taste and see that he's real.

Jesus: The World's Best Evangelist

In the summer of 2008, my wife, Sharie, and I spent several weeks in Kuala Lumpur, Malaysia, building relationships with college students studying in the capital city of a nation that calls itself a Muslim country. "KL," as the city is often called, has become a new locus of education for Asia and the Middle East.

We held a conference hosted by a Chinese/Malaysian church where over six hundred university students attended. We ate meals with them, helped them with their English, and held services complete with worship and preaching. Some of them were followers of Christ, but the majority were not Christians. Surprisingly, they were very open to hearing us speak about our faith.

Among the hundreds of students we met, one young man stands out: a twenty-year-old Hindu man named Richie. He had an amazing afro and an infectious grin on his thin face. And he loved to debate.

He and I ate lunch together one afternoon. Hours after hundreds of other students had left the cafeteria, we still sat across a table from each other arguing for and against Christianity.

After about three hours, we decided to call a truce. I wasn't about to convert to Hinduism and he could never seriously consider Christianity out of respect for his Hindu family, both living and dead. He also said he wasn't convinced that Jesus had risen from the grave.

"So if someone could prove to you that Jesus was really raised from the dead, would you become a Christian?" I said.

"Of course. I would follow a man who defeated death, the greatest enemy. But you could never prove to me that Jesus is alive. I would have to see him. I believe that he lived and died. But not that he lives today."

Richie wasn't ready to be reborn that afternoon. There was no way I could prove to him that Jesus was raised from the dead.

The next day, I preached my final message at the conference. When I asked any students who wanted to be reborn to stand to their feet and confess their faith publicly in Jesus, I saw Richie's huge afro in the very back row. He was standing up.

I went straight to him at the end of the service because I wanted to know if he understood what he was doing when he confessed his sins to Christ and prayed for Jesus to save him and become Lord of his life.

I still have my journal, where I wrote down what he said:

> In my dream [a few nights ago], Jesus did not say anything to me. He just smiled at me, and he was surrounded by bright light. And in my dream, I just knew that he loved me so much. He made me feel very safe and calm. I had peace all over my body, and all my fear and anxiety went away. Then after we talked at lunch, he came back to me again that night and I felt his love again. Then when you asked us to be reborn, I felt warm and loved, and I knew that he really was alive.

Who better than the actual resurrected Jesus to come and prove to a Hindu in Malaysia that Jesus was really resurrected from the dead?

The following day, a small group of us toured KL, and Richie asked if he could tag along. He asked question after question about how he could be a lifelong disciple of Jesus. He also immediately wanted to know how to tell his Hindu family he'd been saved by Jesus. Then he asked me if we could pray together for his family to become followers of Jesus too.

Who better than the actual resurrected Jesus to come and prove to a Hindu in Malaysia that Jesus was really resurrected from the dead?

When Christ calls us, he wants to rescue us. Come into our hearts. Take control of our lives. Make us a new person. Change us from the inside out. Become our Friend and Savior and Lord. These are all different ways of saying the same thing: we can be reborn.

The Darkness of Night

I want to revisit one small detail of Richie's story that centered around two themes: the night and the light.

There was a darkness over Richie's life. He couldn't comprehend the gospel. It was dark in his mind. At night, in the darkness, Jesus revealed himself. He was surrounded by light. The light was stronger than the night. Jesus turned the light on and Richie could now see.

Think of how this parallels your life. Each of us has fought to comprehend things beyond our understanding. As they say, you don't know what you don't know, right? You can't fully understand all the mysteries of God. But don't let that stop you from knowing what you can know about God.

In other words, you don't have to stay in the dark when it comes to God and salvation. If you want to better understand God, to know how he feels about you, to comprehend what he thinks about you, to be convinced that he's real and that he loves you, just look at Jesus. That's when the light comes on.

There was another man who understood the night and the light, and his encounter with Jesus is the genesis for what we know as being "born again." His late-night talk with Jesus, recorded in John 3, is ground zero for the whole idea of being reborn.

If you want to understand God, to know how he feels about you, to comprehend what he thinks about you, to be convinced that he's real and that he loves you, just look at Jesus.

Jesus can turn on the light in your life. No matter what kind of darkness you've faced or may be living in right now, it's no match for the illuminating power of Jesus. Being reborn is like someone turning on the light in a dark room. You can finally see.

A Man Who Had It All

There was an air of excitement throughout ancient Palestine as the Passover holiday fell upon the city once again. Traditions were relived and parties were thrown across Israel, but there was nowhere like the holy city.

Like Times Square on New Year's Eve, Jerusalem was at the heart of the Passover festivities. If you were an Israelite, it was the place to be. The holiday was, and still is, as paramount to the Jewish people as Easter is to Christians.

At Passover, Jews gather to remember how God liberated them from captivity in Egypt and used Moses to deliver them as a nation after hundreds of years in exile as slaves.

To fully understand the significance of the holiday, we have to travel to its roots, which we find in the book of Exodus. When the "all-powerful" Pharaoh refused to free God's people from slavery, God plagued Egypt with a series of incredibly unfortunate events. Soon enough, both the Hebrews and the Egyptians would discover that it was God, not Pharaoh, who was all-powerful.

Exodus 11 sets the stage for the final plague that became the first Passover. After Pharaoh refused yet another of Moses's demands to free God's people, the Lord sent one final detrimental blow. That night, God would take the life of the firstborn sons and animals of every household in Egypt—with one exception. God commanded Moses to tell the Jews in Egypt to mark their door frames with the blood of a sacrificed lamb that night. That sacrifice would serve as their protection, and God would "pass over" their homes and their families, sparing them from death.

That first Passover was pivotal to the freeing of the Jewish people from slavery and their eventual return home, an act of salvation that hinged on sacrifice, bloodshed, God's grace, and faith. Sound familiar? It's a foreshadowing of the perfect Sacrifice to come.

A Tug toward the Light

The Passover would've been familiar to Nicodemus, a man we're introduced to 1,500 years later. Nicodemus was a member of the Sanhedrin, the ruling religious council of his day. Think congress, but without a separation of church and state. He would have been like a senator or the head of the House Intelligence Committee. He had great power. He was an expert in religious law. Nicodemus was also fully aware of everything the Passover celebration entailed.

Yet despite all of that knowledge, Nicodemus didn't have all the answers. None of his training had prepared him for the radical events unfolding around him that Passover season, all of which centered around Jesus. Nicodemus had to see this man for himself.

Just before meeting Nicodemus, Jesus had arrived in Jerusalem for the Passover and entered the temple. He was outraged by what he saw as money changers ripped off poor Jewish worshipers, selling them "acceptable" animals for sacrifice and pocketing the profits. Jesus famously turned over their tables and drove them out of the temple courts with a whip (John 2:13–24).

I believe this event motivated Nicodemus to go find Jesus. He was most likely an eyewitness that day. He saw Jesus enraged at the injustice that had crept into the temple, and he had so many questions he wanted to ask him. But Nicodemus wasn't just an ordinary man. His job was to judge individuals like Jesus.

It was very early in Jesus's ministry, but the rumors were already spreading about this miracle worker from Galilee. Every good Jew was waiting and praying for the Messiah. Could this be him?

It was the responsibility of the Sanhedrin to investigate such rumors and verify or deny them. They would send a delegation in such cases, so that "two or three witnesses" could corroborate or crush the story. That's why it's so odd that Nicodemus came alone to see Jesus. How would it look for Nicodemus to be seen fraternizing with Jesus, a man who flipped tables and talked about destroying the temple?

His reputation meant everything to him, but something was pulling him toward this man, and it was worth risking his good name and position to go find him. But just to be safe, he would pay him a visit at night. When it was dark.

We do the same thing. We use darkness to cover our curiosity, to disguise our deeds, or to hide our indiscretions. It's our nature. When we're afraid others might see us doing something embarrassing, we do it in the dark. But in the dark, don't we also feel a compulsion toward the light? Haven't you felt a tug toward Jesus?

The Light

John 3 tells us Nicodemus went to meet with Jesus under the cloak of night, using darkness as a cover. Don't miss the major significance of this.

The darkness here reached far deeper than the night sky. The night enshrouding Nicodemus was a mirror image of the darkness inside of him, both of which were about to be confronted by the light of the Son.

Time and time again, John uses imagery that contrasts darkness and light. For example, John 1:4 tells us that "in him was life, and that life was the light of all mankind." John was Jesus's closest personal friend. He knew him personally, intimately. His description of Jesus as the light of all humankind was purposefully placed at the beginning of his eyewitness account of the life of Christ.

John continues, "The light shines in the darkness, and the darkness has not overcome it" (v. 5). While the NIV and several translations use the word *overcome* here, we can gain a fuller perspective by looking to the original translation. The

Greek word used in verse 5 is *katalambano*, which means "to comprehend or attain."

Think about trying to navigate your house in the middle of the night because the power has gone out. You can't see the couch or tell the difference between a table or a recliner. In the same way, John sets the tone for his personal account of Jesus and Jesus's interactions with people employing the dichotomy of "the night" and "the light." That makes sense paired with John 1:9–10, which sets the stage for Jesus's ministry: "The true light that gives light to everyone was coming into the world. He was in the world, and though the world was made through him, the world did not recognize him."

Those verses come to life just a couple of chapters later when Nicodemus used the darkness as a cover to come face-to-face with the light. He couldn't make out who Jesus really was. He recognized something in him, a kind of light, but he couldn't comprehend it yet. The Spirit was drawing this wealthy religious expert directly to Jesus.

This was scandalous: the rich religious professional who had it all humbled himself by seeking out a young man with no pedigree, no formal training, and no religious résumé.

Looking for Answers

Breaking with tradition, Nicodemus came alone, without a delegation of witnesses. Maybe, in the dark, no one would see him. But Jesus saw him. He was ready and waiting.

Nicodemus approached Jesus with diplomacy.

"Rabbi, we know that you are a teacher who has come from God. For no one could perform the signs you are doing if God were not with him" (3:2).

Jesus answered bluntly and went straight at his heart. He always does.

"Very truly I tell you, no one can see the kingdom of God unless they are born again," Jesus answered (v. 3). But why on earth would Jesus tell him to be *reborn*?

In Judaism, there were six ways to understand the concept of being "born again," but not a single one of these applied to Nicodemus in that moment:

1. When a gentile converted to Judaism
2. When a husband and wife married and became one flesh
3. When an ordained rabbi completed his formal education and took up his official position as a teacher of the law
4. When a man was crowned as king of Israel
5. At the *bar mitzvah* when a Jewish boy turned thirteen and became a man in the eyes of the community
6. When a rabbi became so respected and honored that he was named the head of his own rabbinical school*

Jesus had to be talking about something altogether different. So Nicodemus responded with, "How can someone be born when they are old? . . . Surely they cannot enter a second time into their mother's womb to be born!" (v. 4). What Jesus told him to do was impossible.

The notion of literally returning to the womb he came from and being born a second time as an adult was absurd. But that wasn't what Jesus was saying.

Jesus continued, "You should not be surprised at my saying, 'You must be born again.' The wind blows wherever it

---

*Robby Gallaty, *The Forgotten Jesus: How Western Christians Should Follow an Eastern Rabbi* (Grand Rapids: Zondervan, 2017), 136–37.

pleases. You hear its sound, but you cannot tell where it comes from or where it is going. So it is with everyone born of the Spirit" (vv. 7–8). Now we see what was drawing Nicodemus to Jesus all along! It was the Holy Spirit, the Third Person of the Trinity, who is still calling people to be reborn today.

In that breath, Jesus was offering Nicodemus a new life, in spite of the good life he seemed to already have. He was using an earthly concept, birth, to describe a heavenly concept: rebirth.

Having achieved "born again" status on his own in the traditional Jewish sense made it hard for Nicodemus to accept that he needed to humble himself and let grace do the work of salvation. The same is true with us. The hardest thing to do is to humbly admit that we actually need what Jesus has to offer. Our thought process goes like this . . .

Why surrender control to Jesus when I can make it just fine on my own?

I have everything I could ever want without becoming religious, so why would I want to change things now?

Why would I want to be reborn when I'm pretty sure I was born okay the first time?

Still in the dark, Nicodemus asked, "How can this be?" (v. 9). Despite all his head knowledge, Nicodemus didn't have heart knowledge. He was twelve inches from being reborn, the distance from his head to his heart. He had verses and facts about God in his head. But Jesus wanted him to open his heart to God, who happened to be standing right in front of him.

To be reborn means to be born of God. As in God gives us a new life. A fresh start. A new identity.

Nicodemus struggled to comprehend this truth but he wanted to understand. He was willing to ask questions. And in the midst of his darkness and doubt stood Jesus. The night and the light, face-to-face.

Jesus didn't force Nicodemus to believe or scare him into submission. On the contrary, he got real with him: "'You are Israel's teacher,' said Jesus, 'and do you not understand these things?'" (v. 10).

Believing in Jesus and accepting the life he offered was a choice that fell squarely on Nicodemus's shoulders. Until he understood who Jesus was and allowed the light to pierce the darkness, he would remain under its veil. So Jesus left Nicodemus with the truth and a decision to make: Would he believe?

Jesus gives each of us the same choice. No one can believe for you. It's your decision. Jesus won't force his way into your heart. On the contrary, he will pursue you, listen to your questions, and care for you, just to prove to you that he loves you. But believing and receiving that love is up to you.

The key to rebirth and eternal life is simply to receive the light and believe in the Son. As Moses gave the people the law of God, it was that same law that demanded blood for the forgiveness of sin. Jesus would die under the law, shedding his blood on a cross, to liberate those who would believe in him from the burden of the law. They could live in God's family. They could start over. They could be reborn.

We don't have to pay our way in, work our way in, or sweet-talk our way in. We just have to believe, to put our faith in the person of Jesus Christ.

This same gift is on offer for us today. We don't have to pay our way in, work our way in, or sweet-talk our way in. We just have to believe, to put our faith in the person of Jesus Christ.

Reborn

To a man like Nicodemus, who seemed to have it all, Jesus's words were groundbreaking.

Aren't they the same to us today? Our words, our actions, our past, our mistakes, and our social status all define us. When we hear the gospel, it's almost too much to comprehend; it seems too good to be true. But what if it is true?

When we come face-to-face with the blinding light of grace, it's almost as inconceivable as crawling back into our mother's womb and being born a second time. Yet it's what Jesus offered Nicodemus, and it's the same free gift Jesus offers us today.

The light is better than the night. Only Jesus can turn the light on for us to see.

A Changed Man

We don't know for certain when Nicodemus fully put his faith in Jesus. But we know he encountered Jesus that night, and it changed everything for him. How can we tell?

Nicodemus comes up two more times in the Gospel of John. First, when the Sanhedrin is calling for Jesus's arrest, Nicodemus tells them to first hear Jesus out before condemning him. Now openly defending Jesus, he wants his colleagues to get the same opportunity to hear Jesus that Nicodemus had received (7:51).

The last time we see Nicodemus is just after Jesus's crucifixion, when he purchases expensive burial spices and helps one of Jesus's followers named Joseph of Arimathea to prepare his body for burial.

What a bold contrast to the man who slipped out to meet Jesus in the middle of the night! With seventy-five-plus pounds of myrrh and aloes to help wrap the body for the tomb, he was now blatantly, boldly identifying himself, in broad daylight, as one of Jesus's followers (19:38–42). That is the definition of being reborn. His night was turned into light.

By no coincidence, immediately after Jesus's encounter with Nicodemus comes arguably the most famous verse in the Bible. And it offers the answer to every reason that could ever hold you back from being reborn.

"For God so loved the world that he gave his one and only Son, that whoever believes in him shall not perish but have eternal life" (3:16).

The Light of the World loves you so fiercely that he gave his life as a sacrifice for you. The God who breathed life into your lungs endured the greatest suffering imaginable for the chance to breathe eternal life into you.

"Whoever believes" includes you and me, even in the depths of our darkness. Even when we think we have it all, we don't have what we need until we have Jesus. Wherever we are, whatever questions keep us up at night, he has the answer. In fact, he *is* the answer, and he isn't remotely afraid of our darkness or our doubts.

Here's the beautiful thing that happens when we encounter Jesus: while we may come to him with questions and confusion, we don't have to leave that way.

With a saving knowledge of Christ comes the assurance of his promises.

In other words, you and I never again have to settle for "I don't know" when we're reborn, because we're the children of a God who longs to know us and be known by us. We don't have to wonder who he is, or where we stand with him, or if he loves us.

So reach out to Jesus. He won't turn you away. Jesus isn't afraid of your darkness. He's already defeated it.

TWO

What to Do When You Don't Belong

I've had so many interesting conversations on airplanes, and it's no wonder. I started flying in 1990 and haven't stopped since. With over a million miles under my wings, I've sat beside some unforgettable folks.

I listened to a mafia boss talk about how to take out your competition in the garbage business, a really ancient man who escaped a Russian gulag in Siberia, and a fascinating fellow who was convinced *The Matrix*, the movie with Keanu Reeves, was reality and we were all living in it.

But nothing tops the conversation I had with Robin from Montana.

Now here's a confession: I get really excited when I have an aisle seat, the captain announces that the door is closed and we're ready for takeoff, and I look beside me only to find that the middle seat and the window seat are empty! I know as a pastor I'm supposed to enjoy talking to people, and trust me, I do. But to get a short nap in or to get another four hundred words done on my next book is such a wonderful little treat.

My plan was working perfectly. I had the row all to myself as we flew from the West Coast back east. I was already drifting off to sleep when someone literally climbed over me. I could feel them step over the top of the seat, placing their hands and feet on the armrests, and shaking my seat but attempting to not touch me. I was resolute to *not* open my eyes, and I kept telling myself that if I didn't make eye contact they would leave me alone.

As the person settled into the window seat, a female voice spoke in my direction, "I hope I didn't wake you up."

Great. A talker. Stick with the plan. Don't respond.

"I tried to climb over you without waking you up. It looked like you were sleeping. I don't see how people sleep on planes. You were out before we even took off."

Even better. A woman who loves to talk so much that she doesn't even need me to talk back. Pretend you're in a coma, Clayton.

She continued, "I love window seats. I get to see the clouds and the ground with all the rivers and lakes and mountains. I barely made this flight. I was running like crazy to make it. Gosh, I'm burning up. Are you hot? They were closing the door when I got to the gate. Thankfully that lady told them to hold it for me. So, where are you heading today?"

Really? Wow. She could go on like this all morning. Maybe I can tune it out. The sound of the engines can mask her voice.

Undeterred by my silence, she reached across the middle seat and shook my elbow. "Hey, are you okay? You seem like you don't feel good. Are you passed out?"

She wins. I give up.

In a hushed tone, I replied, "Sorry, I've been fighting something for a while and was trying to get some rest. I'm okay, just exhausted."

"Well, my name is Robin. I live in Montana, at least for now. I'm heading to New York. I work for a computer software company and . . ." This went on for about ten minutes. She didn't take a breath, I kid you not. She was more than an extrovert. Something else was going on, and I began to pick up on it. She seemed anxious, fidgety, and desperate for human interaction.

I'd seen this kind of behavior before: fingers that can't be still, eyes darting back and forth, clothing constantly being readjusted. I wondered if she was an addict. I began asking her simple questions about her life, her work, her friends, and where she came from. And she unloaded it all, talking as fast as words would flow. Then she got to the hard part and began to cry.

And yet, more than just darkness, there was a spark, a light that refused to go out. She was fighting. Clawing her way forward. Talking to a stranger on a plane.

"I'm a recovering addict. I've been on and off drugs since I was a teenager. I guess I was trying to numb the pain of being raped and having my dad leave us and then having my mom ignore me because of all the men that came and went. She picked some real losers. They were all supposed to be her boyfriends, but they all wound up in my bedroom after she got too drunk to notice. But they weren't too drunk to notice me."

There was a deep brokenness in her, a sadness that seemed to seep through her pores when she talked about her past. And yet, more than just darkness, there was a spark, a light that refused to go out. She was fighting. Clawing her way forward. Talking to a stranger on a plane.

I asked, "So, tell me about your life now. Do you have kids? Are you married?"

When I asked if she was married, she went from quiet tears to guttural weeping. She buried her face in her hands and sobbed. It was loud. I was aware of how many people around us were watching and listening.

"That's a long story. No, I'm not married. I was. A bunch of times. But not now. Why bother? I have a boyfriend, though. He lives in my house. He's a lot younger than me. He's a seasonal worker. A ski guide in the winter and God knows what the rest of the year. He kind of comes and goes, you know. Probably just using me for sex and a free place to live. But it beats being by myself. I don't do well being alone, so I'd rather have him than nobody."

Such brutal honesty was disarming. She wasn't holding back. She told me the progression of her addiction. It had started with marijuana and gotten worse from there. She went so far as to show me her dental work, a long and expensive process to fix her teeth that had rotted from the drugs.

Then the conversation took a turn. She asked, "I'm sorry, I've been talking forever. What about you? What do you do?"

"My name is Clayton and my wife is Sharie, and I'm a minister."

She exploded.

"I knew it! On the outside you look like a bouncer at a bar but you talk and act like a priest or a counselor or something. You're really easy to talk to, and I guess that's why I've been telling you my life story. So, what do you think I should do?"

And there it was. Just like that, the door was open.

Going to the Well All Alone

The best part of Robin's story happens next, but first I want to show you how Jesus changed a woman similar to Robin when she encountered him face-to-face at Jacob's well. We read about her in John 4.

It was sweltering in Samaria at noon, the hottest part of the day.

A group of women in the community of Sychar collected water in the cool of the morning, easing the burden a little bit. It was a daily routine as they caught up with friends and kept up with the news, which tended to include gossiping about any bad behavior of its residents.

But there was one woman who wasn't welcome in their clique.

She'd been married too many times to warrant an invitation to join their group. And why would she bother? She'd seen enough judgmental sideways glances from them. She'd rather keep to herself and steer clear of the well when the other women were there.

After five husbands had come and gone, no one was touching her with a ten-foot pole. Why couldn't she make the men stay? Was she barren? Impure? Diseased? Insane? Definitely unlovable, she thought. What had she done to cross God? Was she cursed? She probably felt like damaged goods.

Think of how we judge a woman who's been married five times today. Add to that the fact that she was currently living with another guy (number six). Now try to imagine her life two thousand years ago, in a small religious community where nothing was secret and no sinful deed could be hidden. Shame must have dripped off her arms like the sweat from carrying heavy water jars during the hottest part of the day.

And what about her current live-in boyfriend? Maybe the sixth time was the charm. Maybe he would be different and would be the one to pick up the pieces and make her whole. Was that too much to expect?

The Samaritan woman had a lot in common with Robin from Montana. A checkered past littered with broken relationships and a bruised soul.

An Unexpected Encounter

The last thing she expected that day was a run-in with a Jewish man at Jacob's well. Yet there he was, smack-dab in the middle of Samaria. At noon. And, by the way, what in the world was he doing there? Jews hated Samaritans. And Samaritans despised Jews.

Their conflict ran deep. Their animosity was hundreds of years old.

In fact, the Jews hated the Samaritans so much that when they had to travel the length of Israel, they took a "shortcut" that added thirty miles to their travels just to avoid stepping on Samaritan soil.

So why was a Jewish man lounging by the well at midday? And why was he looking right at her as she approached the well to draw her water by hand?

Then the man did the unthinkable. He spoke to her.

"Will you give me a drink?" he asked her. With one simple question, he shattered three cultural laws.

First, he was a man and she was a woman, so their conversation was an oddity because men didn't speak to women in public unless they were married. Second, he was a Jew and she was a Samaritan, which meant he automatically thought of her as a half-breed, worse than a gentile. Finally, as if that were not enough, he requested a drink from her. A huge no-no!

Jews looked at the Samaritans as inferior, avoiding them at all costs. The Samaritans, whose ethnicity was Jewish blended with other people groups, were descendants of the lowest class of people left behind after Babylon's conquest of Samaria hundreds of years earlier. They had intermarried with Babylonians and tainted the bloodline.

Out of their blended background arose unique religious practices, the main one being their insistence that Mount Gerizim was the sacred holy place originally intended for worshiping God, rather than the temple in Jerusalem as the Jews believed.

This feud ran so deep that Jews weren't supposed to go to a Samaritan's house or eat or drink from a dish that a Samaritan had touched.

But there was Jesus, sitting casually at the cultural center of Sychar in the heart of Samaria, asking a local woman for some of her water, breaking all the rules.

There was nothing random about his interaction with the woman at the well. Scripture tells us that after Jesus's time in Judea, where he met Nicodemus and began to gain more followers, he was returning to Galilee as the Pharisees were catching wind of his growing popularity, avoiding them as much as possible.

In other words, his departure from the region was guided by a purpose. He headed north to Galilee, but that wasn't the only place he was going. In John's words, "He had to go through Samaria" (John 4:4). But that wasn't geographically true. He shouldn't have gone there at all.

Jesus could've bypassed Samaria like the pious Jews did, taking the thirty-mile loop to sidestep the "deplorable" land, walking around it rather than risking getting close to "those people."

But Jesus doesn't avoid hard situations. Because he loves us, he makes his way into our mess. Regardless of our background or behavior or bloodline, Jesus comes to find us when we need help.

So, instead of taking the loop, Jesus chose to walk right into the heart of Samaria. He *had* to. Because at Jacob's well there was a hurting woman in need of a new life. He didn't care that she was a Samaritan. She wasn't damaged goods. She was his mission. She was the very reason he had to go to Samaria.

> But Jesus doesn't avoid hard situations. Because he loves us, he makes his way into our mess. Regardless of our background or behavior or bloodline, Jesus comes to find us when we need help.

She answered his request for a drink naturally: "You are a Jew and I am a Samaritan woman. How can you ask me for a drink?" (v. 9). Translation: "Are you totally nuts? You know the rules. I can't talk to you, and you can't drink water I've touched!"

Then we're told in parentheses, "For Jews do not associate with Samaritans" (v. 9). The Greek word translated as *associate* here, *synchrōntai*, literally means "no dealings with." In other words, Jesus should have had absolutely nothing to do with her.

But Jesus doesn't see people like we do. We focus on the outside. Jesus looks inside. He identifies the image of God in people, and that's what he values in us. He doesn't judge based on appearances, and he doesn't label based on race or ethnicity. He sees the individual for who they are.

Living Water

Jesus responded, "If you knew the gift of God and who it is that asks you for a drink, you would have asked him and he would have given you living water" (v. 10).

Why was his offer of living water so intriguing to her? Because in the desert climates of the Middle East, access to water meant the difference between life and death. And because there were two types of water: stagnant water that you might find in a pond or a puddle, and living water, which was fresh and free-flowing. You couldn't stomach stagnant water. It made you sick. But living water moved and flowed. You could drink it, and it was a rare commodity in the desert, hence everyone coming to the city center to draw drinking water from the well.

The thought of never having to come to the well again alone also intrigued her. If she could access living water, she would no longer have to trudge to the well in the heat of the afternoon just to survive. Living water would change her life. So she proceeded, "Are you greater than our father Jacob, who gave us the well and drank from it himself, as did also his sons and his livestock?" (v. 12).

She knew what the Jews thought of Samaritans.

Jesus answered with an even more unexpected reply than his previous one: "Everyone who drinks this water will be thirsty again, but whoever drinks the water I give them will never thirst. Indeed, the water I give them will become in them a spring of water welling up to eternal life" (vv. 13–14).

An offer like that was unreal, impossible even, but it was too good to pass up. "Sir, give me this water so that I won't get thirsty and have to keep coming here to draw water" (v. 15).

There was desperation in her request; otherwise she would have never dreamed of having a conversation with a Jewish stranger. I can also hear a note of sarcasm in her voice, as if to say, "Okay, I'll engage you in this nonsense. If you could actually give me my own water source, it would change everything for me. Let's hear what you have to say, but I think you're full of it."

Revelation

"Go, call your husband and come back," Jesus told her (v. 16). If he was going to offer a woman something, especially a gift of value, her husband should be present. But as Jesus knew then, and we know now, she had no husband to summon, only a boyfriend and a string of ex-husbands in her past. Six men in total.

"'I have no husband,' she replied" (v. 17). Imagine the heavy baggage attached to those words. Couldn't she just have one conversation with a stranger who didn't know her reputation? Wasn't it bad enough that everyone in the small town of Sychar knew every detail of her life? Did this Jew come all this way to ridicule her too?

"Jesus said to her, 'You are right when you say you have no husband. The fact is, you have had five husbands, and the man you now have is not your husband. What you have just said is quite true'" (vv. 17–18).

With his response, she realized that Jesus was no ordinary man. How could this stranger know her deepest source of shame?

The good news for us is simple: Jesus knows our background, our bloodline, our bad behavior. And he loves us enough to come looking for us because he has something of great value to offer us.

He's not shaming her. His tone is gentle. He understands. He's not belittling or condemning her. He's speaking with compassion. That's why, instead of running away in shame, she continued to question Jesus, but now moving to spiritual issues: "'Sir,' the woman said, 'I can see that you are a prophet. Our ancestors worshiped on this mountain, but you Jews claim that the place where we must worship is in Jerusalem'" (vv. 19–20).

Who was this man? He'd pulled back the curtain and turned on the lights in her life. So rather than setting herself up for being judged or lectured, she quickly changed the subject. The true place of worship was the most contentious argument she could've picked, and it would certainly redirect their conversation away from her sordid story.

But Jesus was on a mission, so he leveraged her question to reveal his true identity to her.

"'Woman,' Jesus replied, 'believe me, a time is coming when you will worship the Father neither on this mountain nor in Jerusalem. You Samaritans worship what you do not know; we worship what we do know, for salvation is from the Jews. Yet a time is coming and has now come when the true worshipers will worship the Father in the Spirit and in truth, for they are the kind of worshipers the Father seeks'" (vv. 21–23).

A New Perspective

Jesus patiently explained that authentic worship was centered around the motives of the heart, not the geography of her location. He didn't argue with her. He listened. He engaged. Her heart was stirred, so much so that she uttered these words to Jesus: "I know that Messiah [called Christ] is coming. When he comes, he will explain everything to us" (v. 25).

Then Jesus changed her life forever with one simple sentence: "I, the one speaking to you—I am he" (v. 26).

What a surprise! She was waiting on the Messiah to come, and he had come all the way to Samaria just for her.

The Savior of the world broke every rule in the book to get to her. He dignified an undignified woman by treating her with respect. Hundreds of years of racism and inferiority vanished as she, finally, experienced a man treating her with kindness.

Never underestimate the power of the love of God. People are reborn when they experience unconditional love from God, not when they experience self-righteous religious experts beating them down with a Bible. Hearts are opened to the gospel when people see Jesus for who he really is—a man who's willing to sit with an outcast woman in the middle of the day and defy all the protocols just to show her she has value to God.

> **The Savior of the world broke every rule in the book to get to her. He dignified an undignified woman by treating her with respect.**

The Aftermath

You guessed it. The Samaritan woman was reborn on the spot! She put her trust in Jesus as the Messiah. As a matter of fact, she put down her water jar and ran to tell the people in town what had just transpired, urging them, "Come, see a man who told me everything I ever did," and asking in awe, "Could this be the Messiah?" (v. 29).

She was changed in an instant. She no longer cared what anyone thought of her. Her bad reputation was the furthest thing from her mind. She had to tell everyone about this man.

Scripture tells us that when the Samaritans heard the woman's testimony that day, "They came out of the town and made their way toward him" (v. 30).

When someone is that fundamentally changed by Jesus, it's contagious, so people couldn't help but come and see what she was talking about. I think her tarnished reputation made her testimony even more believable. Why would a woman like her risk the rejection of her village by telling them a story like this if it weren't true?

Her boldness led to the salvation of many. John 4:39 says, "Many of the Samaritans from that town believed in him because of the woman's testimony, 'He told me everything I ever did.'"

Her encounter led to their conversion, and as soon as they met him they were even more convinced that Jesus was the Messiah. "They said to the woman, 'We no longer believe just because of what you said; now we have heard for ourselves, and we know that this man really is the Savior of the world'" (v. 42).

In one afternoon, a whole mass of people were transformed from a community of religious outcasts to citizens of the kingdom of heaven. She wasn't the only one who was reborn. Jesus extended grace to her, and she shared it with her people as soon as she could.

Bloodlines

Jesus made the trip to Samaria to make a statement.

Jesus came for women. He came for moral and social outcasts. He came for misfits and half-breeds and the marginalized. He came for villains and vixens and victims of racism. He came for the abused, for throwaway people who didn't have a family or a crew or a clique or a posse or a people.

He came for you and me.

He came for a woman who had probably been divorced and discarded by multiple men because she was barren and could not conceive. He was creating a brand-new family that wasn't based on bloodlines.

And speaking of bloodlines . . . of all the people he could have chosen, Jesus disclosed his identity as Messiah first to a woman, not a man, who in her very body had the DNA of both Jews and gentiles. Her literal bloodline was passed down through a crooked family tree, which is why the Jews hated the Samaritans so much. Their blood wasn't pure. But that was okay, because Jesus's blood was pure enough.

Jesus came for women. He came for moral and social outcasts. He came for misfits and half-breeds and the marginalized. He came for villains and vixens and victims of racism.

She was a representation of the nature of the gospel: Jesus came to call people from all tribes and nations and ethnicities and would make them one family, the church. Her physical body was symbolic of the spiritual body Jesus was creating, one full of diversity.

Robin from Montana

So, what happened with Robin from Montana?

When she asked me what I thought she should do with her life, I knew she was ready to be reborn. What story do you think I used to connect her to Jesus's ability to change a woman's life? The Samaritan woman at the well, of course.

She wept out loud as I told her how Jesus loved this woman, how he wasn't disgusted by her past, and how she became an evangelist to her own people after Jesus changed her.

As soon as I paused long enough to take a breath, Robin said, "How do I do that?"

"Do what?"

"Become a Christian. Get saved. Whatever you call it. I want to do it."

I reached across the empty seat between us and took her hand. I led her in a really simple prayer of repentance, and then I invited her to pray her own prayer. She confessed her sin, told God how sorry she was and how much she wanted to be loved, that she believed Jesus was alive, and that she wanted to start over.

I gave her my email address and asked her to contact me if she needed help or prayer, and to let me know when she found a good church. Not long after that plane trip, she reached out to me.

Her email said,

I feel like a brand-new person. I feel free. The guilt and shame are getting better. I have a lot of work to do. And I found a church! I just went to a random church last Sunday and it was weird, but I loved it. After the service a really sweet woman asked me where I was from. I told her exactly what you said, that I met a preacher on an airplane and I gave my life to Jesus, and that preacher told me I needed to find a church. So here I am.

The woman was the pastor's wife, and she told me she had been praying for a new woman to disciple because the woman she'd been meeting with for several years was moving. So I ate lunch with the pastor's family and now I'm going to be meeting with her every week. I guess God answered both of our prayers!

Here's my point: Jesus doesn't discriminate based on our background, our behavior, or our bloodline. He comes to where we are. He's not afraid to be associated with us. He'll reach out to us when others avoid us. And when we see who he truly is, we automatically change so deeply that we cannot help ourselves. We tell the people we love the most about the Person who changed us and how they can have an encounter with him too.

THREE

When You Have Little to Offer

If you've ever wondered if you can actually make a difference . . .

If you've ever felt like you had nothing to offer God . . .

If you've felt too small or insignificant to truly help other people . . .

Then this chapter will strike a chord deep in your bones.

Just bring what you have to Jesus. Give it to him and watch him show off, because once we're reborn, Jesus will surprise us with the amazing ways he can use what we have in his kingdom.

What Would Jesus Do This Time?

The crowds were assembling as evening drew near, with people coming in droves to see and hear Jesus upon his return to the Galilean region. He'd become a household name there recently.

It was certainly worth a walk to Bethsaida, where he and his followers were rumored to be staying. They'd picked a quiet place to spend their time, off the beaten path; nevertheless, it seemed as if everyone wanted to encounter this man. There were rumors, and there were stories.

He'd cast out demons just across the lake. He'd healed lepers. And he taught with authority. What miraculous signs would he perform this time?

Jesus had risen to such a level of popularity by now that Matthew 14:21 tells us there were "about five thousand men, besides women and children" in the crowd.

If we estimated only one woman and one child for every man present in the crowd, the number increases to fifteen thousand. Now imagine families with multiple children. You get the idea. The crowd easily eclipsed twenty thousand people. And they all came to see Jesus.

Sea of Miracles

Galilee was Jesus's home. It was where Jesus began his ministry by turning water into wine. It was where he called Peter, James, Andrew, and John to drop their nets and become fishers of people, and the place where he beckoned Matthew to leave his tax collecting days behind and become his disciple. It was where Jesus preached the Sermon on the Mount. Rabbis like Jesus could often be found teaching along the shores, using the water to amplify their voices to their students.

Jesus had also just received some bad news. A family member had been murdered.

John the Baptist, Jesus's cousin, had prepared the way for Jesus, proclaiming him as the Messiah to all who would listen.

His growing popularity made him a valued voice of reason among many Jews, but his criticism of King Herod's marriage to his brother's former wife got him beheaded (Matt. 14:6–12).

Jesus's heart was broken.

"When Jesus heard what had happened [to John], he withdrew by boat privately to a solitary place" (v. 13). He needed to get away, to go back home. He wanted to retreat to a quiet place with his disciples. In addition to being fully God, he was also fully human. Tired from travel, sad with grief, he just wanted to rest.

Despite his exhaustion and grief, Jesus took the role of a servant and prioritized the people over his own feelings.

But as soon as the locals heard that he was back, they came in droves. Jesus could've easily turned them away, gotten back on the boat, and left the town for another remote locale where they couldn't find him.

But in Mark's words, "When Jesus landed and saw a large crowd, he had compassion on them, because they were like sheep without a shepherd" (Mark 6:34). Despite his exhaustion and grief, Jesus took the role of a servant and prioritized the people over his own feelings.

A Hungry Crowd

As the day ended, after Jesus had tirelessly blessed and taught and healed people, the disciples urged Jesus to send them all home. Everyone was hungry and tired.

We've all been there—the end of an afternoon at a football game or amusement park. You've walked miles in the blazing heat with children in tow and are now packed in a sea of people who don't seem to be moving anywhere. To top it all off, you and the other twenty thousand people will all be flooding into the same limited number of restaurants. Imagine how the multitudes gathered in Bethsaida felt. As incredible as it was to be in Jesus's presence, stomachs were growling.

So Jesus turned to Philip, one of his twelve disciples, and asked him, "Where shall we buy bread for these people to eat?" (John 6:5).

This was impractical and impossible. Imagine the thoughts that must have run through Philip's head at that moment! Jesus wanted them to do *what*?

Impossible is where Jesus does his best work. Are you facing an impossible situation? Something you can't fix? A problem you can't solve? Then you're in the perfect position to see Jesus perform a miracle, because a miracle doesn't happen until there's a mess that demands one.

> **Are you facing an impossible situation? Something you can't fix? A problem you can't solve? Then you're in the perfect position to see Jesus perform a miracle, because a miracle doesn't happen until there's a mess that demands one.**

Philip answered practically, "It would take more than half a year's wages to buy enough bread for each one to have a bite!" (v. 7).

Philip completely missed the point. It didn't add up. He was thinking about the math. He should have thought *miracle*. Math is what we do. Miracles are what Jesus does.

When Jesus questioned Philip, he wasn't looking for a solution. *Jesus was the solution*. Jesus was testing Philip's faith to prove and strengthen it. John 6:6 lets us in on a little secret, saying that, "[Jesus] asked this only to test him, for he already had in mind what he was going to do."

Philip might've failed the test, but he still got to witness the miracle.

Before Jesus even had a chance to respond, another of his disciples, Andrew, announced to Jesus, "Here is a boy with five small barley loaves and two small fish, but how far will they go among this many?" (v. 8).

While Philip was still formulating the bread-to-earnings ratio it would take to give each member of the crowd a crumb, Andrew spoke up with a little more faith. Even as he approached Jesus, though, Andrew had doubts.

Andrew believed. And he doubted. Just like you and me.

Both often live side by side: trust and doubt, faith and fear. Two competing feelings try to occupy the same space in our heads and hearts. What Jesus wants for us is to simply trust him, to choose faith over doubt, even when we can't possibly know how he will work it out. But isn't that what faith is, really? Believing God will come through when we have no clue how.

Andrew wasn't sure how a couple fish and a few loaves of bread would feed the masses, but in that place where his doubt and faith lived together, Jesus did the impossible.

Isn't this a picture of us? We live in the tension of being certain and being unsure. We want to trust God fully, but we also feel the fear in our stomachs. We have moments where our faith wins out, and other times when our doubts are stronger.

Childlike Faith

Among the twenty thousand, a little boy emerged from the crowd with his lunch in hand. There he was, standing before Jesus, offering what little he had.

This kid had to be hungry. He could have eaten his Jewish Lunchables, but he put the little he had into Jesus's hands, trusting it would do far more good there than in his own.

He gave Jesus all that he had. It seemed like a little, but it was actually a lot.

Jesus took his two little fish and five loaves and turned them into enough food to nourish every person in the crowd. Everyone ate until they were full, and there were even twelve baskets of leftovers when it was all said and done, all because a little boy showed everyone what Jesus can do with what we give him.

I can't help but notice the contrast here. Philip was filled with doubt. Andrew had a mixture of doubt and faith. But the boy was all faith! That Jesus picked a child to teach his disciples about faith was itself a miracle.

That's the point. A child taught the disciples. A little faith goes a long way.

Already in Mind

Mark 6:34 tells us Jesus cared tenderly for the crowd. He wanted to feed them himself, but not just physically. Jesus wanted them all to know he was the Messiah. His feeding of the masses was deeply symbolic, as it mirrored Moses feeding the Israelites with manna in the desert after the exodus from Egypt. This was another sign Jesus was fulfilling to show himself as the Savior they had been waiting for.

Jesus already had in mind what he would do the moment Philip approached him. He had spotted that little boy in the crowd and knew that he would use him to teach his disciples about faith, showing how much more he could do with a little than they could do with a lot.

God used a little boy with a little bit of food and a tremendous amount of faith to feed not tens of thousands, not even millions, but billions of people. *Because two thousand years later, we're still talking about an unnamed little boy's encounter with Jesus.*

This means Jesus can use *you.* It doesn't matter how old or qualified or wealthy you are. It doesn't matter what your name or past is, or how small you are. The people Jesus chooses to use are the ones with hearts big enough to take him at his word.

It's the ones close enough to him to hear him ask the question, "Where will we find enough bread to feed all these people?" It's the ones who answer, "Here, Jesus. It's all I have, but you can have it."

From Stuttering to Strung Out

My friend Chris Dew is one of the most effective preachers I've ever heard. But he wasn't always leading people to Jesus. Before he was reborn, he was strung out and hopeless. He reminds me of the boy who gave his lunch to Jesus. It seemed so little, but Jesus used it to do a lot. Here is his story, in his own words.

> "My name is C- Ch- Chr-," I stammered as my heart raced and the shame crept in.
>
> Constant stuttering and anxiety made my life a living hell. Every morning started with a new plan of how I was going to make it all day without embarrassing myself. Where could I go to eat where I could write my order down? How can I get out of that class where the teacher makes us read out loud? This went on for years.

I spent most days in an exhausting attempt to hide my stuttering problem. One day, after failing miserably, some guys asked if I wanted to smoke weed with them. I didn't get high the first time, but the next time I did and I loved it.

I'd found my answer! The emptiness in my soul subsided and a smile leaked to my face. I felt okay in my own skin for the first time in my life. Smoking weed soon became an everyday escape. It became my source of happiness and peace.

I declared that weed was the only drug I'd ever do, but it was a slippery slope. New relationships gave me access to any drug I desired: Adderall, Xanax, shrooms, acid, Klonopin, cocaine, Hydrocodone, ecstasy, Oxycontin, and eventually heroin. I began selling weed to pay for the harder drugs. I not only had an answer to emptiness, but I also found purpose and identity. I was the guy with the best weed. But this new identity as a dealer cast a dark shadow.

What started out as a means of treating my emptiness quickly turned into a cancer that was destroying my life. I knew I needed to stop or I wasn't going to see my twenties, so I checked myself into a mental hospital. The exit ramp wasn't nearly as enjoyable as the on-ramp.

The First of Many Attempts to Pump the Brakes

I was sixteen years old, and my first attempt at freedom from heroin had landed me in Holly Hill Mental Hospital.

As I looked around the white-walled prison, the other patients were a vision of my future. Hollow humans trapped internally and externally against their will. I had never felt anything this terrible! Desperate cravings, intense rage, and constant complaining led the doctors to pump me full of psychiatric tranquilizers that made me feel like a zombie but did nothing to fill the void or take away the withdrawals.

After three days of hell, I raced out the doors, and the glaring sun irritated my eyes like warm vinegar had been splashed in them. My parents and I had a handful of medical records with pages of

WHEN YOU HAVE LITTLE TO OFFER   61

official jargon that ultimately said, "Chris is a drug addict." How insightful. I left the hospital and immediately got high.

The Death Needle

When snorting heroin no longer had the same effect, I started using a needle, which brought new levels of euphoria. And destruction. After the first stick, everything in my life turned three shades darker. Heroin was my god and I served it faithfully, but the object of my affection was out to kill me.

Life was a roller coaster of the highest of highs and the lowest of lows. The most epic feelings of intense pleasure were followed by the darkest feelings of desperation. The external consequences were also devastating. I couldn't keep a job. My body was sick. Many of my friends overdosed and died. Legal issues. Stealing. Gang violence. Robbing and being robbed. Car wrecks. My life was a mess. And it was about to get even worse.

The Worst Day of My Life

"BEEP BEEP BEEP BEEP BEEP." My dad's alarm clock went off in the other room. The annoying sound was muffled enough to not wake a sleeping heroin addict for many hours, but loud enough to annoy me after my eyes finally unlatched. I looked at my clock: 10:00 a.m. Shouldn't my dad be at work by now? He must have forgotten to shut off the alarm.

I'd just moved back in with my dad after a two-month stint in North Carolina that didn't turn out so well. I'd moved away with hopes of starting a new life, but the darkness followed, just like each time before. I had turned the new place into another living hell. I was glad to be home again with Dad.

He was my rock. Whenever I was in any kind of trouble, financially, legally, or medically, he always came to the rescue. He was my best friend.

I stumbled through the living room. When I hit the threshold of my dad's room I had an eerie feeling that everything was about to change.

I walked to the other side of the bed, and terror rushed through my body. "Dad! DAD! DAD!" Tears rushed down my face as I shook him and begged him to wake up.

Nothing.

I called 9-1-1.

Emotions ripped through my body. He'd had a massive heart attack and had been dead for hours.

This was the most alone I'd ever felt. This was not a game. This was final.

What part had I played in this?

I was put in charge of his estate and given way too much money for a twenty-year-old junkie to manage. Within eighteen months, I had spent nearly everything and had destroyed the lives of many people around me. I finally broke.

The End and the Beginning

A week before Christmas, my mom graciously invited me over for dinner, knowing I probably hadn't eaten in days.

"Chris, aren't you done yet? You're twenty years old. Your dad's money is almost gone. Your stripper girlfriend almost died twice this week. Is this the life you want?"

I didn't answer immediately, but blurry images of distant hopes flashed through my mind. This isn't what I wanted for my life.

"Do you want to give life one more chance?"

I'd been to treatment many times before. What would be different this time?

"I guess."

We walked upstairs and began to search online for affordable drug treatment.

"Look, there's one in New York."

My mom had obviously never experienced heroin withdrawals. "Too cold."

"How about Florence, South Carolina?"

That's pretty close. Fairly warm. "Okay."

It's amazing the admissions director could understand me through the tears and stammers.

"We'll see you tomorrow," they said after nearly an hour of broken conversation on the phone. My mom and I hugged longer than we had since I was a little boy.

I walked out the door into the cool December night, went straight to the ATM, cleared my account, and called the dope man. If this was the last time I was going to get high, I was going to go out with a bang.

A New Place and a New Season

When we arrived at the treatment center the next day, I stood nearly six feet tall and weighed one hundred pounds. Fresh track marks from dirty needle pokes crowded my skeleton-like, tatted arms. The drugs had become ineffective at filling the gaping hole in my soul that I had felt since I was a boy. As we pulled up the gravel driveway to the rehab facility, my palms began to sweat. "Why did I agree to this again?"

I stumbled out of the car, still feeling the effects of the three bags of heroin, a couple bong hits, and the last dozen or so Xanax and Klonopin. I had nowhere else to go and no more strings left to pull.

There was no life in me; I was a walking dead man! The whole reason I started using drugs in the first place was to fill the void I felt inside, but somehow drugs had actually intensified this longing. I was hopeless and empty; and I had been for as long as I could remember.

The Knock I Was Waiting For

"Do you want to go to church?" one of the residents asked.

Why would I want to go to church? I didn't belong in a place like that. But I would get to leave the rehab for a few hours. Maybe there would be cute girls there.

"It's Christmas Eve, c'mon!"

As we walked into the church I felt out of place, but quickly made my way to a seat as the service started.

"Do you feel like you're too messy for God?"

"Does nothing you've tried seem to fill the emptiness in your soul?"

"Do you want a fresh start to life?"

The speaker's words penetrated my heart. He talked about Jesus as a real Person. He explained how God loves broken people and that he made a way for people like me to be forgiven and changed. I knew I needed it.

I made the decision to give up my old life completely and place my trust in Jesus Christ. I sobbed as I prayed with a tall guy with a bright red beard. I got a taste of the joy I'd always wanted. It felt like pure jubilation, but perfect and divine. What I had been looking for wasn't more drugs, sex, or money; it was God.

I encountered Jesus and I was reborn.

Now, Chris is a dear friend and brother to me. He travels the country telling his story of how an encounter with Jesus changed everything about his life. He's seen thousands of people put their faith in Jesus for salvation.

"I got a taste of the joy I'd always wanted. It felt like pure jubilation, but perfect and divine. What I had been looking for wasn't more drugs, sex, or money; it was God. I encountered Jesus and I was reborn."

As I was finishing this chapter, he texted to tell me that sixty-six students were saved at a summer camp where he was preaching. I get texts from him like this all the time, because all he does now is tell people how to be reborn.

Like a boy with very little to give Jesus, Chris gave what he had. He gave Jesus his sin and his life, and Jesus gave him a rebirth. And like the boy's little lunch fed the multitudes after it was broken, Chris's story of brokenness turns to life-giving bread every time Jesus uses it to set someone free with his grace.

What do you have that seems small, insignificant, or broken? Have you told yourself that God can't use you?

Your mess is an invitation for his miracle. Watch what he can do with what you have.

If you're alive, God is not done with you. Whatever is in your hand, whatever is in your past, whatever keeps you up at night, give it to Jesus. Your mess is an invitation for his miracle. Watch what he can do with what you have.

FOUR

What to Do When You've Blown It

Part of being reborn is being retrained.

Many of us have been conditioned to believe that Jesus is on the lookout for sinners, and when he catches one in the act, he drops a nuclear bomb of judgment on our head. Is Jesus up in heaven keeping a ledger or a spreadsheet of every wicked thing we've done, every curse word we've said, every link we've clicked on, and every sinful thought that's ever entered our mind?

I have good news: nothing could be further from the truth.

A Black Woman Saves a Klan Member

"There's a Klansman in the crowd!"

Imagine what would happen if someone shouted those words in a public place. Maybe the grocery store or a sporting event or a Christmas parade. The word *Klansman* conjures up images of men in white hoods and robes, of burning crosses, of hatred and racism. We all know what the Ku Klux Klan is, and we know what they stand for.

I've never heard anyone yell, "There's a Klansman in the crowd," but Keshia Thomas has.

Keshia is a black woman. In 1996, she was an eighteen-year-old high school senior in Ann Arbor, Michigan. On June 22, the KKK had planned a public march in her town. Keshia joined a much larger group of protesters who were there peacefully opposing the Klan.

The police were there, geared up with body armor and tear gas, to maintain a controlled environment while protecting a small group of Klansmen. The members of the KKK were decked out in their infamous garb: high, cone-shaped hoods and white robes. The police had built a safety fence to separate the anti-KKK demonstrators from the Klan members, and Thomas was on the other side of the fence.

Then a woman with a megaphone shouted, "There's a Klansman in the crowd."

People began to shout "Kill the Nazi," and the white man began running. Members of the crowd who had gathered, however, stopped him, knocking him to the ground. Several people in the crowd started kicking him and hitting him with the wooden placards of their signs. The situation was escalating.

Wearing a Confederate flag on his clothing, and with what appeared to be Nazi SS tattoos, this white man in a largely African American crowd was an easy target. As the mob mentality began to take over, and more people joined in the kicking and beating, something came over Keshia Thomas. She told the BBC, "When they dropped him to the ground, it felt like two angels had lifted my body up and laid me down."[*]

*Catherine Wynne, "The Teenager Who Saved a Man with an SS Tattoo," *BBC News*, October 29, 2013, https://www.bbc.com/news/magazine-24653643.

The African American teenager threw her body on top of the man, Albert McKeel Jr., shielding him from the blows of the crowd. A student photographer named Marc Brunner captured the heroic act on camera. The pictures seem to stop time in its tracks as you can see the white man on the ground, helpless, receiving a barrage of blows. You can see the passion on Keshia's face as she apparently screams at the crowd to stop. When I look at the pictures, I see another emotion on her face as she saved McKeel's life: pain.

Later Keshia would give the reason that she risked her life to save a man who, for all she knew, could have been a member of the KKK. "I knew what it was like to be hurt. The many times that that happened, I wish someone would have stood up for me."

Because she had suffered pain in her life, there was an immediate empathy that welled up in her heart. Almost involuntarily, lifted by angels, she moved to his defense. She stepped in and literally laid her life down on top of this man, willing to take the pain that was aimed at him.

I type these words from the study in my home in South Carolina, the state where I was born, the first state to secede from the Union over the issue of slavery. The city where I was born, Charleston, was the location of the first shots of the Civil War. That same city witnessed one of the most heinous acts of racism and violence in modern American history when Dylan Roof murdered nine African American Christians inside their church in June 2015. He later confessed that he killed them in hopes of igniting a race war.

There's no limit to the cruelty of human beings who think they are superior to others.

And yet there is more than just darkness in us that rises up. There is also light. A spark of the divine. We were crafted by our Creator, and the blueprint he used was himself. So for every heinous act of evil we hear about, there are ten acts of love and kindness that go unnoticed. For every Dylan Roof who takes a life, there is a Keshia Thomas who risks her life to save another.

> *We were crafted by our Creator, and the blueprint he used was himself. So for every heinous act of evil we hear about, there are ten acts of love and kindness that go unnoticed.*

When I first saw the pictures of Keshia throwing her body on top of the man with Nazi SS tattoos, shielding his face with her hand, my mind went back to a similar scene that occurred when a self-righteous mob of religious professionals dragged a woman they were ready to kill before Jesus. And he stepped in to save her.

If you've ever blown it big-time, and wondered if Jesus still loves you . . .

If you've doubted whether or not Jesus can forgive you for that one thing . . .

If you've asked yourself if you were worth saving in the first place . . .

Keep reading.

Red-Handed

Imagine the scene with me from John 8.

Jesus was positioned in the holiest place on earth, the Temple Mount in Jerusalem.

He was teaching from a scroll of the Old Testament when the crowd began to stir. There was a commotion. People started to stand up and point. It looked like the Pharisees were coming. They were easy to spot because of the religious regalia they wore in public. They loved being seen.

It became clear that they had someone in tow. It was a woman, clutching a small garment to her breasts, trying to conceal her body that is barely covered. All but naked, she sobbed in despair, for she knew their intention. They would kill her just to prove a point.

It seems she was caught in the act of adultery. Presumably she was a Jew. She was having sex with a man who was not her husband when the Pharisees burst through the door. "We got you! Caught you red-handed. Come with us. You're going to the temple." They started dragging her toward Jesus.

"The teachers of the law and the Pharisees brought in a woman caught in adultery. They made her stand before the group" (John 8:3). This mob of religious bullies brought her front and center into the temple and placed her in the midst of the crowd assembled there. They "made her stand," indicating their power, their ability to push people around, to force them to go where they dictated. They were motivated by power. They'd had control of all things religious—until Jesus began teaching the people.

As the crowds began to flock to Jesus, they'd felt their tight grip over the people begin to loosen, and they just couldn't let that happen. So we see over and over again in the four Gospels their attempts to trick and trap Jesus by baiting him into doctrinal debates and theological arguments. This, however, was another level.

I can't prove how this all went down, but my theory is simple. These men had been watching Jesus, so they knew exactly when they could find him teaching in the temple courts. They also knew who this woman was. Maybe they'd heard she was sleeping with another man, and they planned the moment when they would catch her in bed with him. Or maybe the man was married and she was a prostitute. It was still adultery, even if he was the only one who was married.

Either way, she was expendable.

I think it was a setup. Were they waiting outside in the bushes? Were they huddled in another room? Was the man in on the whole thing? Was the man a Pharisee himself? There was no limit to how far they would go to shut Jesus up and get rid of him, even to the point of setting up an expendable woman to face the death penalty for adultery.

Deuteronomy 22:22 and Leviticus 20:10 (the law they claimed to follow) clearly state that in the case of adultery, both the man and the woman are to receive the punishment. The obvious question, then, is, Where was the man? Did they pay him off? Did he slide on his clothes after the deed was done and slip on down to the temple to watch the show?

One thing is certain: the woman was the only one who was publicly shamed and humiliated. She alone was facing death.

Jesus Won't Be Bullied

In reality, it's not the woman the Pharisees wanted to kill. It was Jesus.

The Pharisees were heartless. They didn't care about the woman.

The Pharisees were hypocrites. They didn't care about the law.

The Pharisees were power hungry. They only cared about prestige and platform.

As they approached Jesus, their chosen spokesman took the opportunity to quote the law of Moses in front of the crowd, absolutely certain they had finally found a way to catch Jesus in blasphemy. If they could do that, they could discredit him once and for all and end his rise to prominence.

If Jesus agreed with them, then the woman would be stoned to death and they would have established their authority as the true leaders of the Jews in the face of this strange man from Galilee.

If Jesus disagreed with them, they would have public proof that he was a blasphemer who didn't follow the law or submit to their father Moses.

The half-naked woman who stood helpless in the temple courts represents you and me as we stand before God with nothing to cover us. We are guilty of sin. We have said things and done things that have broken God's law and deserve to be punished. In some sense, we see ourselves in her story: accused, ashamed, and needing rescue.

Grace on Display

But Jesus steps in—for her and for us. He refuses to bring the hammer of God's justice until we've had a chance to experience mercy. This mercy has rightly been explained as us not receiving the punishment our deeds deserve. But this woman's encounter with Jesus also gives us a beautiful glimpse of something else. We see God's grace on display.

If mercy is what happens when we don't receive the punishment we do deserve, then grace is what happens when we get something wonderful we don't deserve. The woman caught red-handed received mercy when Jesus granted her a stay of execution. The same woman received grace when Jesus acquitted her of her crime and gave her the gift of forgiveness she hadn't earned at all.

> *If mercy is what happens when we don't receive the punishment we do deserve, then grace is what happens when we get something wonderful we don't deserve.*

And that is the essence of grace: getting something good that we don't deserve.

How could Jesus suspend God's justice and let her off the hook?

Jesus knew that there was a Roman cross of crucifixion in his future, and that he would die there in her place and ours, taking the punishment we all deserve for all the sins we've committed. That's why he could liberate her without hesitation. It's why he refused to play into the hands of the Pharisees and their attempt to entrap him. It's why he bent down to the ground and scribbled in the dirt.

What Did He Write on the Ground?

What Jesus said next forced all the men to drop their stones and leave the temple: "Let any one of you who is without sin be the first to throw a stone at her" (John 8:7). I think it was his words, as well as what he did when he stooped down to doodle in the dirt, that sent them away.

Everyone wants to know what Jesus wrote when he put his finger on the ground. There are some strong theories out there from some really smart people.

Maybe he wrote down the names of the Pharisees along with the names of the women they'd slept with in the past. Was he pointing out to them that he knew what they'd done and they also deserved punishment?

Maybe he was writing down other specific sins they'd committed. Was it an amount of money one of them had stolen from the temple treasury? Was it a date from years earlier when one of them had paid for a prostitute and assumed no one would ever know?

We'll never know what he wrote. However, we hear echoes of the Old Testament in this story. Remember, the Pharisees spent their lives studying the Old Testament. They had large portions of it memorized. Their eyes were trained to pick up on symbolism and meaning as they connected everything back to their Scriptures. They thought themselves experts in the law. But they had met their match with Jesus.

He knew the Scriptures better than they did. He was the Author. They studied it, but he wrote it.

As he stooped down to write with his finger, the stone floors of the temple courts were covered with dust.

Now see this imagery in that moment as you read Exodus 31:18: "When the LORD finished speaking to Moses on Mount Sinai, he gave him the two tablets of the covenant law, the tablets of stone *inscribed by the finger of God.*"

Do you see it? The finger of God had touched stone tablets and written the law for Moses to give the people over one thousand years earlier. We call them the Ten Commandments. Now Jesus places his finger on the stone floor of the temple and gives us something better than rules to follow. He gives us grace.

He's saying in that moment that he is God, that he wrote the law with his finger and gave it to Moses. It was Jesus who came to complete that law by living the perfect life none of us could ever live and dying the death each of us deserved, doing so in our place so that we could be free from sin and liberated from shame.

God in flesh was touching stone with his finger again that day. And the Pharisees picked up on exactly what Jesus was saying.

So it really doesn't matter what he wrote on the ground. The fact that he extended his finger to the stone floors of the temple would have immediately been recognized in the context of Exodus 31 as Jesus's claim that he was God and that he had the right to forgive this woman they wanted to kill.

But that wasn't the only thing Jesus was communicating with his finger. He was also pointing to (or maybe even writing out) Jeremiah 17:13, which says, "LORD, you are the hope of Israel; all who forsake you will be put to shame. Those who turn away from you *will be written in the dust*, because they have forsaken the LORD, the spring of living water."

Did you catch that? Jesus knew that the Pharisees knew this passage. They knew that when he put his finger on the dust-covered stones of the temple floor, he was symbolically writing their names in the dust, connecting them to the words of the prophet Jeremiah. This was Jesus indicting them as the ones who had turned away from God. He was acting as prophet that day, declaring that just as someone would come through the temple and sweep away the dust from the stone floors, they too would soon be swept away, never to be remembered because of their pride and self-righteousness.

Let's not miss the forest for the trees here: this story is about Jesus saving a woman's life. He rescued her. She was dead until he stood up to her executioners.

This story is about Jesus saving a woman's life. He rescued her. She was dead until he stood up to her executioners.

And in this story, we see ourselves. We are that woman, caught and shamed with no defense to fall back on but a thin hope for mercy. And as Jesus saved her in John 8, he would go on to save countless millions who would rely on his grace as their hope of forgiveness and salvation.

Jesus Is Our Salvation

We all cheer when Jesus stood up to the religious bullies and shut them down while telling the woman to go and leave her life of sin behind her. And yet, I can't help but think that Jesus not only cared about the one about to be killed but also about the killers. He cared about the mob of men holding stones. He wanted to set them free too.

Jesus cares for wives who have been beaten and berated by abusive husbands. He also cares about those husbands. He wants the wives to be rescued. He also wants the husbands to encounter salvation so they will stop hurting others.

Jesus cares about children who have been neglected by materialistic parents or assaulted by sexual deviants. He wants to rescue those children from those people, but he also wants to save and change the parents who neglect them and the adults who assault them.

Jesus cares about African Americans who have felt the sting of racism, who have been targeted for no reason by authorities, or who have been called names that we dare not even utter.

And Jesus also cares for the racists who hate minorities. He cares for the KKK members and wants to save them from the bondage of hate.

So, as we celebrate the grace that Jesus extends to victims, we have to wrestle with the fact that Jesus also extends grace to victimizers, abusers, the self-righteous, the proud, and the would-be killers.

So, as we celebrate the grace that Jesus extends to victims, we have to wrestle with the fact that Jesus also extends grace to victimizers, abusers, the self-righteous, the proud, and the would-be killers. He saved a nameless woman that day from death. He's still saving people from spiritual death today.

A God-Moment in Gatlinburg

In January 2019, I got a Facebook message from a guy who claimed we'd met years earlier. His message said,

> Clayton I believe that I have a story you may want to hear. I met you about 20 years ago in Gatlinburg, TN. You had been eating at a restaurant and got sick and left. As you crossed the road, you ran into a long-haired guy that you prayed for on the spot. That guy was me, but I am a completely different man now that the Lord Jesus has changed my life. I am now an ordained minister. I cannot wait to tell you my whole story.

I remembered it vaguely. It was January 2000. We were hosting our Crossroads Winter Conference in Gatlinburg when I left a meal at a restaurant feeling sick. That was when I met Jason on the street.

And this is his story, in his own words.

Twenty years ago I was a different person than I am now. Revisiting the past is difficult because it's hard to believe the person I once was.

The thoughts I had on a daily basis had consumed me to the point that I had plans in place to kill someone. It was almost like an evil spirit had taken over.

I grew up with my great-grandparents in an old shack with an outhouse. My uncle also lived with us. He died at twenty-three in a car accident. Soon after, my great-grandmother and great-grandfather died. A few years later my mother died of a brain aneurysm. I turned to death metal. I listened to bands that described mutilation, murder, and perfect crime. It fueled my passion for death, and I became obsessed with committing the perfect crime.

During this time I went on a weekend trip with my wife to Gatlinburg. She'd become so concerned for my state of mind that she told all our relatives how afraid she was of what I might do. As we walked up and down the streets we met a guy trying to get us to take a time-share tour in exchange for $100 cash at the end of the tour. But we had to come back a week later for the tour.

The following week my wife and I headed back to Gatlinburg for the $100 but the man in the booth was nowhere to be found. I was beside myself in anger. My wife knew I was about to do something drastic.

Pacing back and forth, I saw a big guy with a bald head walking across the street. I was so angry I yelled at him, asking if he knew anything about the guy in the booth. The guy kept walking toward me and I was thinking "I will stab this guy in the neck if he gets much closer." He came straight at me and got in my space, but I just stood there frozen. I couldn't understand why I allowed this guy to get so close to me. He asked me what was wrong and for some reason I told him. Then he put his hand on my shoulder and looked at me right in my eyes and began to speak with concern as if I was his friend.

He asked if I would wait for just a moment then he left and came back ten minutes later with almost fifty kids and explained that he was on a youth retreat and was at a restaurant eating, and he had gotten sick and had to leave. He said when I yelled at him, the sickness left.

Then the youth group gathered around me in a big circle, and he said there was a young lady that wanted to give us money to help us. They held hands and then the big dude asked me if he could pray for me. I didn't want to have anything to do with Jesus. I surely didn't want him praying for me, but to just show thanks I allowed them to pray.

This guy knew SOMEONE. He began to pray about my desire to kill someone and how I was tormented inside. I never told him this. He spoke with such authority and peace at the same time. This all struck a nerve in me and I broke down and began to cry in front of all these kids.

This man invited us to a youth event where he was preaching that night in Gatlinburg. We drove around Pigeon Forge the rest of the day debating on going back. We finally went. A band called Disciple was playing a concert. The lead singer preached during the show. I met him afterward and he invited me to his church, which was really close to our house. As if all that wasn't enough, that youth group that prayed for me earlier saw me and came to talk to me. They seemed to really care about us.

A few weeks later we visited that church. It was not like anything I'd ever experienced. It was exciting and full of love. The pastor preached a message that was just for me. I ran to the altar. There was someone behind me praying and crying over me. It was the lead singer of the band that had invited me to the church a few weeks earlier. He prayed with me and I met Jesus personally that night.

The Lord has miraculously given me peace where I used to be tormented. The stranger in the street of Gatlinburg has been a mystery to me for years, but last night (1/7/19) I realized it was Clayton King.

A Salvation That Keeps on Saving

Jason is now fighting cancer and diastolic heart failure. He has stage 4 non-Hodgkin's lymphoma that's in remission. He's trusting God for healing. Until he dies, or until Christ returns, he intends to keep telling his story of how Jesus saved him from taking a person's life, and how Jesus saved his.

Remember Keshia, from the KKK rally? She risked her life to save a man who looked like her enemy. Jesus risked his life to save the life of a woman who was caught red-handed in adultery. And God used multiple people to save a man who was hell-bent on killing an innocent person just so he could say he'd committed the perfect crime.

Jesus cared about Klan members who wanted to hurt black people. He cared about Albert McKeel Jr. with his Nazi tattoos. He cared about the woman who was about to be stoned to death. He cared about the men who wanted to kill her. He cared about Jason that day in Gatlinburg.

And Jesus went to great lengths to save them all.

Just imagine all the things he's done to save you.

FIVE

Reverse the Curse in Your Life

I was born in 1972, just a few months before abortion was legalized. My birth mother couldn't raise me alone and didn't trust that my biological dad would be there to support a family. She chose adoption for me, and it saved my life.

My adoptive parents always told me how special it was to be chosen. When they both died eighteen months apart (my mom died in late 2010, and my dad died in June 2012), I knew nothing about my origins but was determined to find the family I came from. And with the help of Facebook, a DNA test, and some good friends from my church, I located my biological family within a matter of months.

For the first time, I learned about my great-great-uncle Furman, who was born in 1860.

After the Civil War, many emancipated slaves had no choice but to stay in the homes they'd been living in, with no better place to go and no better options. One of these former slaves, well advanced in years, was named Plent Rogers, and he was all but blind. He had a strange daily ritual. He would feel his way out to an old oak tree and pray to God. Out loud.

It seems that young Furman, about ten years old, was a menace with a mischievous streak. He saw Plent going to the tree every day to pray, and even followed him at a distance to listen to him.

Furman went to the old oak one day, well before Plent had stumbled there to pray, and climbed to the top. His plan was to wait until Plent paused in his prayer and then speak to him from the top of the tree with a booming voice, as if he were God. But before he had the opportunity to pull off his prank, he heard Plent Rogers pray for him.

The old man was asking God to speak to young Furman and to save him from his sins so that he could know the love and forgiveness of Jesus Christ.

And sitting there in the top of that big oak tree, a young man with little more than mischief on his mind had an encounter with Jesus. He was saved *in that tree*. And just like it is for us, that moment when he encountered Jesus for the first time was just the beginning of his salvation.

Reverend Furman Hezekiah Martin graduated from Southern Seminary in 1891 and went on to pastor churches in Virginia and North Carolina, as well as serving as a trustee at the Baptist Orphanage of Virginia. Older relatives of mine said that when he would travel to preach, people would flock to hear him, and they would also flock to the altar to give their lives to Jesus when he gave the invitation for people to be saved.

Uncle Furman had his first encounter with Jesus while he was sitting in a tree. That's a strange place to start a relationship with God, don't you think?

It doesn't matter where you are when you meet Jesus. It could be a bar or a biker rally or a Baptist church. It's not about where you start your relationship with Christ, it's about where he takes you once you meet him.

It's not about where you start your relationship with Christ, it's about where he takes you once you meet him.

A Wee Little Man

The name Zacchaeus means "pure," but when we first meet him in Luke 19, he certainly doesn't seem pure. Anyone who knew him would have said he was dirty, corrupt, and vile. Truth be told, he was one of the most hated people in all of Israel, and for good reason.

He worked for the IRS.

Okay, it wasn't exactly the Internal Revenue Service, but it was the corrupt equivalent.

Zacchaeus was a tax collector, and he was evidently good at it because he was rich. He was in charge of a number of other tax collectors. Simply put, he was like a mob boss who took a cut of all the money the loan sharks working underneath him collected. That's what it means when Luke calls him a "chief tax collector" (Luke 19:2).

It makes sense that people wouldn't like him because he took their money, but it was worse than that. He was a Jew and collected taxes from other Jews, but he worked for the Romans.

The Roman Empire was the definition of wickedness, debauchery, and sexual excess. They celebrated the very things that the Hebrew Scriptures forbid.

The Romans broke the first commandment by worshiping all sorts of gods and by displaying their images publicly. The Jews believed in one God and were forbidden to make any images of God. The Romans used to accuse the Jews of being atheists because they couldn't believe that an entire nation would have only one deity while Rome had thousands.

When the Romans invaded Israel in the first century BC and established their military dominance, they set up governors and an army to enforce the peace of Rome, desecrating the Holy Land with their gentile presence. An entire guerrilla force called the Zealots formed for the purpose of driving the Romans out of Israel, killing them one by one, revolting in large numbers, and hopefully ushering in the Messiah who would restore the glory of Israel.

The Romans who occupied Israel with brute military power forced the Jews to pay for their occupancy in the form of taxes. These taxes paid for Roman soldiers' salaries, housing, food, and training. They paid for rulers like Pontius Pilate to live in luxury. They paid for the conquests of other lands. They also paid for the Caesars to live in opulent palaces, where they hosted weeklong parties filled with every conceivable vice.

Every single Jew knew their taxes were funding the evil empire, but they were powerless to do anything about it because the ruling council, the Sanhedrin (Pharisees, Sadducees, scribes, and the high priest), was colluding with Rome in order to keep its power.

The Romans had a fancy way of recruiting tax collectors. They employed local folks: men who knew the culture, understood who was who, and had networking capabilities. They didn't want honest men with integrity. They wanted cutthroat criminals who were greedy and calculating.

The fact that Zacchaeus was a "chief" among tax collectors meant that he had risen in the ranks among the worst, most despicable men in all of Israel to a place of managing other greedy tax collectors. This man was a traitor to his people.

And how did he get rich? The Romans demanded a certain amount from the tax collectors annually, but they allowed them to take as much as they could from peasants, farmers, and business owners. Whatever they collected above the specified amount, they kept for themselves. Extortion, threats, and corruption were rampant.

Zacchaeus was living large in his big house, counting his money. He should have been happy, right? Then why did he climb up a tree to try to get a glimpse of an itinerant preacher from Galilee?

Because there's no amount of money that can fill the God-shaped hole in our hearts. There's no achievement that can give us inner peace. There's no accomplishment that can give us lasting joy. Bigger houses and bigger bank accounts just lead to bigger disappointments. We were created by God, for God, to know God, and all the other pursuits we chase after eventually let us down. So we symbolically climb up trees to look for something real.

Up a Tree So He Could See

Zacchaeus was curious and he was short, so when Jesus passed through Jericho, he had to climb up a tree to get a glimpse of this man whom everyone was talking about. No doubt the crowd didn't want to let him skip to the front row. He had to shimmy up a sycamore fig tree.

Jesus does indeed come his way and sees him up in the tree. Then, in a turn of events no one expected, he called him by name to come down from the tree, and then invited himself to the home of Zacchaeus (Luke 19:5).

The crowd couldn't believe that a rabbi like Jesus would debase himself by entering the home of a notorious sinner, even sitting at his table and eating his food.

What Is It about Trees?

The Bible is full of trees, and they have a surprising amount of symbolism. The concept of cursing and blessing in association with trees goes all the way back to the very beginning, in the garden of Eden.

Adam and Eve eat fruit from a tree in Genesis 3 and they fall under the curse of sin.

Deuteronomy 21 states that anyone who hangs from a tree is under a curse, speaking specifically of a form of punishment for capital offenses in Judaism. The apostle Paul wrote, "Christ redeemed us from the curse of the law by becoming a curse for us—for it is written, '*Cursed is everyone who is hung on a tree*'" (Gal. 3:13 CSB).

Jesus came to earth to reverse the curse. He actually *redeems the tree* from being an object of cursing to being an object of blessing. And how does he do it?

He dies on a tree.

He takes on our sin on a tree. He becomes the curse and is nailed to a tree. He strips the curse of its power and makes the tree of crucifixion a symbol of our salvation. The first

Christians used this language because they had seen it with their own eyes.

Peter preached the gospel to the high priest in Jerusalem only days after the resurrection and said, "The God of our fathers raised Jesus, whom you killed *by hanging him on a tree*" (Acts 5:30 ESV).

Peter, proclaiming the gospel to Cornelius, said, "And we are witnesses of all that he did both in the country of the Jews and in Jerusalem. They put him to death *by hanging him on a tree*, but God raised him on the third day and made him to appear, not to all the people but to us who had been chosen by God as witnesses, who ate and drank with him after he rose from the dead" (10:39–41 ESV).

A tree was the source of our greatest curse in the garden of Eden, and a tree was the setting for our greatest salvation on Golgotha.

A tree was the source of our greatest curse in the garden of Eden, and a tree was the setting for our greatest salvation on Golgotha.

Finally, in the new heaven and the new earth, we will all be given the right to eat from the Tree of Life, as all of creation is restored by God at the end of days.

Jesus says, "Look, I am coming soon! My reward is with me, and I will give to each person according to what they have done. . . . Blessed are those who wash their robes, *that they may have the right to the tree of life* and may go through the gates into the city" (Rev. 22:12, 14).

Zacchaeus first encountered Jesus while he was up a tree, one he climbed by using his hands and feet. Jesus would hang from a tree by his hands and feet as they were nailed through the wood with rusty nine-inch-long spikes.

Now you understand the powerful meaning behind the moment when Jesus looked up in that tree and called Zacchaeus to come down. He was calling him away from his sin, away from the curse, to a better life, to hope and freedom and salvation. The man who would soon hang from a tree on Golgotha came to Jericho that day to get Zacchaeus out of a tree.

So, when Jesus invited himself over to hang out, there was no argument from the short little chief of tax collectors. It had probably been a while since he'd had any friends over for dinner. If he even had friends.

Jesus is naturally drawn to us when we're lonely, isolated, and seeking. When we're searching for something worth living for, we can bet that Jesus is what we need, and he's already got his eyes on us. He knows what trees we've climbed in our quest for meaning and identity, and he's going to get us down, one way or another.

Zacchaeus welcomed Jesus into his home, and before the day was over, he welcomed Jesus into his heart.

Here and Now

Don't ever underestimate how much a small act of kindness can affect someone. Your willingness to stop and notice someone, to ask them how they're doing, or to ask them if you can pray for them could be a small catalyst that begins a domino effect of change in their life.

It's easier than you might think. An invitation to lunch. A cup of coffee and some conversation. A hand on a shoulder, eye contact, a compliment and an encouraging word. You have the power to lift someone up without breaking a sweat.

When we acknowledge someone, we dignify them. When we're not ashamed to be identified with them, they feel empowered and valued. When we call them by their name, like Jesus did, we ascribe value and worth to them.

This is precisely how Jesus reached the most hated traitor in all of Jericho. He noticed him. He called him by name. And when no one else would so much as smile at him, Jesus asked Zacchaeus if he could come over and hang out with him at his house.

So while the religious illuminati were fuming over Jesus and his dinner date, Zacchaeus was having an encounter with Jesus that wrecked him almost instantly. He was so utterly undone by the presence and power of Christ that he stood up and made a bold, public declaration. "Look, Lord! Here and now I give half of my possessions to the poor, and if I have cheated anybody out of anything, I will pay back four times the amount" (Luke 19:8).

Now that Zacchaeus has encountered Jesus, he realized he'd been chasing the wrong win. Wealth won't work once you've seen God in the flesh.

This is the most bold and believable act of repentance in the entire New Testament because it's so immediate. He was convinced of the supreme value of having a friendship with Jesus, to the extent that he liquidated his assets on the spot. Don't you just know the Jews were lining up to take him up on his offer to quadruple what he'd stolen from them?

But Zacchaeus didn't care. Money was meaningless once he'd met the Messiah. The irony is almost laughable; he started his day wealthy and ended his day bankrupt, but he'd never been richer than when he gave away everything to follow Jesus.

The Setup and the Contrast

If you read straight through the Gospel of Luke, you'll see how he highlights outsiders and those on the margins. Luke was a medical doctor, so he had a trained eye for detail. He was also a gentile, so he was sympathetic to the people who didn't have a Jewish pedigree. That's why he recorded so many stories of lost people, hurt people, and even hated people like Zacchaeus.

But to really understand how Zacchaeus was reborn when he encountered Jesus, go back one chapter and read Luke 18. There are two significant things that set up this surprising story of salvation.

First, Jesus tells a parable where he described a "holier than thou" Pharisee with an arrogant attitude and a proud posture. Who did he tell the parable to? "To some who were confident of their own righteousness and looked down on everybody else" (v. 9). Jesus doesn't back down from conflict, and he's not scared to pick a fight with religious bullies, right? Jesus has guts.

Jesus told this parable specifically to arrogant religious leaders and highlighted one such religious hypocrite in the story he told. As the fictitious man prayed, he had the audacity to thank God that he wasn't like the tax collector who happened to be standing near him. The self-righteousness just dripped off him!

But then, in a surprising twist, the despised tax collector actually prayed too, but he had a posture of humility toward God. "But the tax collector stood at a distance. He would not even look up to heaven, but beat his breast and said, 'God have mercy on me, a sinner.' I tell you that this man, rather than the other, went home justified before God. For all those who exalt themselves will be humbled, and those who humble themselves will be exalted" (vv. 13–14).

Then a few verses later, in Luke 18:18–30, we read about a real encounter that took place when a rich young man who ruled over a vast estate asked Jesus about gaining eternal life. Much like the Pharisee, he was arrogant and bragged that he'd kept all of the law perfectly since he was a young boy. His posture was proud, and when Jesus challenged him to give away his wealth to the poor in order to follow him, he flat-out refused.

Do you see the setup? Jesus flipped the script and showcased the humility of a tax collector in contrast to the smug arrogance of the wealthy and the religious. The young rich guy refused to give up his stash of cash in chapter 18, but rich tax collector Zacchaeus didn't even have to be asked to part with his wealth in chapter 19. He volunteered. He encountered Jesus and was reborn. He freely offered to walk away from his wealth because he'd found something more valuable: salvation.

And it all started in a tree in Jericho.

We're always looking for something bigger than ourselves. We're wired to know there's something more, something eternal that will outlast us. We want to find it, to know it, to experience it. But it's not an "it" we're trying to find. It's a "he," and he wants a relationship with us.

The Old Man under the Tree

My wife and I started a nonprofit ministry in the mid-1990s, and for twenty-five years we've hosted a huge event, Crossroads

Summer Camps, with over five thousand teenagers in attendance. We've seen thousands of teenagers give their lives to Jesus and experience salvation at Crossroads.

Their stories capture my heart, as do the stories from our camp staff.

In 2018, one of our summer staff members shared a story about her father, Ravi, and how he witnessed a miracle in a village in North India. Later, she kindly connected me to her father via email, and I was able to get the story from him in more detail. It brings to mind the story of Zacchaeus because it features, of all things, a tree.

Ravi was working as a civil engineer in Singapore when God called him into ministry. One day, as he prayed in Singapore, he sensed a call from the Holy Spirit to go to Gujarat, a state in North India. He was born in South India and had never been to Gujarat. He didn't know the language or the culture. He actually didn't know anyone there. But he began to pray that God would lead him to a "man of peace" when he arrived at his destination. He prayed Matthew 10:11, "So when you go to a town or a village, find someone worthy enough to have you as their guest and stay with them until you leave" (CEV).

A month later, with no plan and big faith, Ravi reached the village of Bhuj with a translator who spoke the local language. He placed a map of Gujarat on a table, asking God where, specifically, he and his translator should go. Here is his story, in his own words.

> As I was praying I saw the word *Thurmbo* in flashing lights, and this repeated over and over again. So I looked up the word and it was the name of a remote village sixty kilometers away. The only way there was a bike, which would take us nearly four hours.

I thought I would just go to that place and do a prayer walk around the village since God has strongly hinted this place to me. Then I would return back to Bhuj. So I went there. It was very hot and humid. I found an old man sitting under a huge tree, so we went to talk with him. He asked me who I was and why I came to his village, and I replied that I was Ravi from South India. The old man assumed I was from the government. After about ten minutes of having a general talk about his family, he asked me once again about why I was there. This time I told him that I came here to develop the village but at the same time share about God.

As a civil engineer, Ravi was able to travel freely throughout India and Singapore to plan development for rural areas. But as he spoke to this elderly man under the tree, he sensed this was the man of peace and influence he had asked God to lead him to.

The old man got a little tense and asked which god I wanted to talk about.

I replied "Yeshu Mashi," which is Jesus Christ. He started screaming "Yeshu Mashi!" over and over, and I was very scared because I had no clue what he was going to do to me. My heart was beating fast and I was thinking that maybe today is my last day of being alive. I asked him why he was angry, and he started sharing a story that went back twenty years.

He said that very morning, after breakfast, he'd fallen back asleep and had a dream that two men came to his village to share about Jesus that day. Then he woke up and asked his sons, who were at home, if anyone was there to talk about Jesus. They told him no one was there and to go back to sleep.

Unable to go back to sleep, the old man remembered an incident that happened twenty years earlier. While he was still a young man working on his farm, a missionary came and shared the gospel with him. But he was enraged, kicked him, and told him to get off his farm. He didn't want to hear about a foreign god in his Hindu land. The missionary was physically injured and left that village immediately. No other Christians had come until my translator and I came that day. When the old man remembered how violent he was with the missionary twenty years earlier, he was convicted and felt very guilty for what he did.

The translator told me the people in that area believe in dreams. They believe they will really happen. So when he dreamed that two men were coming that day to tell them about Jesus, then we came there, he knew it was true.

> "Before I even went to share the gospel, God had been there, even twenty years ago. The only thing I had to say was Jesus Christ, and the rest was taken care of by God."

So I shared the gospel with him, and on that day thirty-two people, which was his whole family including his five sons and their wives and their children, all accepted Jesus Christ and got saved. It was amazing to see how God spoke to me before I went to the village, guiding me to the exact place. God also knew exactly how to touch the old man since this village believed in dreams. Before I even went to share the gospel, God had been there, even twenty years ago. The only thing I had to say was *Jesus Christ*, and the rest was taken care of by God.

Jesus found an old man in a remote village in India when he was under a tree. Jesus found a little boy in the Deep South in the late 1800s sitting in the top of a tree. Jesus found Zacchaeus when he was up a tree. And he pursued each of them because he wanted them to be reborn.

It doesn't matter what kind of tree you're in or under. Jesus is looking for you. He's after you to take away the guilt and shame, to undo years of regret, as if you were literally born again, a second time, with a brand-new life ahead of you. In Christ, you can really, actually be reborn.

SIX

Reaching Out to Jesus

From 2006 to 2012, I spent the equivalent of four months in the hospital with my dad. It was spread out over years—a week here after a heart cath, two weeks there after a triple bypass. Along with my mom and brother, I took turns staying with him as he recovered from all the bad things that happen when you're in your sixties and you have heart disease and diabetes.

I slept in different places all over the hospital during those long nights while I watched my dad slowly succumb to the ravages of age and disease.

One night I was twisted up like a pretzel on a couch in the cardiac ward lobby when a guy about my age walked in around midnight. The waiting room was completely dark, but there was a light on down the hall. I saw a dimly lit, mysterious figure approaching me. Then softly, almost humbly, he said, "Hey, are you Clayton King?" Evidently he'd heard me preach at Newspring, the church his family attended.

I stood up to shake his hand, removed my earbuds, and turned on a lamp so I could see his face. He said his name was Shannon Forest.

I told him that I'd been in the cardiac ward with my dad for over a week and we hoped he'd get to go home soon. Shannon said, "I'm up here with my dad too, but it doesn't look like he's going to get to go home."

"What do you mean? Isn't he going to make it?" I said.

Shannon told me that they'd just called him and his mom into the room to inform them that his dad was dying. His vital organs were shutting down. It was only a matter of time. They needed to think about end-of-life issues. Shannon had just left the room where they had that discussion and was taking a walk around the hospital to muster up some courage and pray.

That's when we bumped into each other. Two young men, praying and hoping for healing. Both of us there because we loved our dads.

Right there in that dark lobby, we put our hands on each other's shoulders and prayed for our dying dads.

I don't remember praying very long. But I do remember us asking God for a miracle. We asked our heavenly Father to heal Shannon's earthly father, which seemed impossible. I gave Shannon a hug and wished him well, and he left.

He was about to return to the room to tell them to remove his father from life support.

Seven Years Later

Over the years, I would remember praying with Shannon, but other than the memory of us praying for his dad, I assumed he went back to the room that night to tell the doctor and the nurses to take his dad off life support and allow him to die naturally.

Seven years later, I was standing in line in a sporting goods store, about to buy a new pair of baseball cleats for my son, when a man tapped me on the shoulder from behind. "Hey, you probably don't remember me," he said when I turned. "I'm Shannon Forest and we met once in the hospital."

I immediately knew who he was. "Of course I remember you. We prayed for your dad. My dad made it home, but he and my mom have both died since I saw you in the hospital." Then I said, "Shannon, I am so sorry about your dad."

He replied, "Oh, you don't know?"

I didn't know.

"You thought he died? He didn't die, Clayton. God healed him. He's still alive today."

What. Did. He. Just. Say?

So he told me the story, standing in a checkout line as my son stood beside me and held a pair of cleats.

Seven years earlier, he'd left the waiting room and gone back to his father's room where nurses were waiting. Fully prepared to pull the plug, he entered the room to find everyone with dumbfounded looks on their faces.

While we were praying in the waiting room, his dad's vital signs changed. His organs began functioning again. His heart rate increased, and he showed signs of life.

Two weeks later his dad walked out of the hospital. I finally met his father seven years later, when our church did a video story of his miraculous recovery.

All of this happened while we were praying. In the lobby. For a miracle. For God to save his dad. While we were praying, God was working.

Did it ever even occur to us that God might actually do what we asked him to do? Or was it more like a spiritual reflex, an instinct, a deep and almost automatic spiritual response to a crisis so dire that mere mortals couldn't hope to change it?

God is still healing people. His power hasn't waned or weakened over the years. And while I have no idea exactly how prayer works, I do know this: prayer only works if we actually pray. And the reason prayer works is because God works. While we're praying, God is always working, even when we don't see it.

While we're praying, God is always working, even when we don't see it.

Three Desperate Situations

Mark 5 tells us how Jesus once faced three crises in a row: a man possessed by demons, a father with a dying daughter, and a woman who couldn't stop bleeding.

The energy was electric in Capernaum when Jesus and his disciples arrived there by boat. It was a familiar place.

Just across the lake, you could hear a man screaming all night long as he cut himself with stones, possessed by demons. With inhuman strength, he tore through every shackle placed on him. But when he encountered Jesus, he was changed. People were rattled, to say the least (Mark 5:1–20).

One moment this man was completely unhinged. The next he was sitting at the feet of Jesus, dressed and in his right mind for the first time anyone could remember. Just hours earlier he had been running back and forth through a Jewish graveyard, something strictly forbidden by Hebrew law. He'd been out of his mind, or at least out of control of it.

The deranged, naked guy who'd spent his days and nights among the tombs slicing up his own flesh with rocks was now fully clothed and coherent, telling everyone who would listen about the man who saved him, claiming he was the Son of God.

It was like he'd been reborn. His encounter with Jesus saved his sanity and his life. After seeing that kind of radical transformation, the people's collective interest was officially piqued. Word spread that Jesus was back in Capernaum, just across the lake.

As soon as Jesus and his followers got off the boat, Jairus, the local synagogue leader, met him on the shore. His twelve-year-old daughter was on the brink of death, and Jairus was in desperate need of a miracle. If Jesus could heal a demoniac, he could heal his daughter. But before Jesus and his followers could get to Jairus's house, they had to go through the massive crowd of people who came to see Jesus. Then he encountered the third person needing a miracle.

He faced three hard situations. Three people in crisis. And he cared for each of them.

Jesus is never too busy to care about us. While he lived, he always took time to see people and to serve people. He's listening to every prayer you pray, even as he superintends the details of the universe. Since he is God, he doesn't get tired of our requests for help, healing, or assistance.

Twelve Years of Unanswered Prayers

Despite his celebrity, Jesus didn't have bodyguards. There were no ropes to cordon the crowds from his path. Instead, true to his nature, he stepped right in the middle of the masses.

But Jesus wasn't the only one fighting the crowd that day. There was someone else, and she was immersed in two fights: one to get to Jesus, and one for her very life.

Out of the hundreds, maybe thousands, of people pressed together, one woman's story stands out.

"And a woman was there who had been subject to bleeding for twelve years. She had suffered a great deal under the care of many doctors and had spent all she had, yet instead of getting better she grew worse" (Mark 5:25–26).

Have you ever had a nosebleed that seemed like it would never stop, no matter how much pressure you applied? Or have you ever accidentally cut yourself in the kitchen or the garage, or scraped your knee or elbow, and you just couldn't seem to stop the bleeding?

Imagine bleeding without end for twelve years. That's the amount of time you spent in first through twelfth grade. It's four years of college, three times. In other words, it's a long time for a person to bleed. And it's the amount of time the woman in the crowd that day spent suffering. She woke up every single morning for over four thousand days, praying for God to heal her.

I can't help but notice that Jairus's daughter, who was dying, was twelve years old. This nameless woman in the crowd had been bleeding for twelve years. So Jesus came to Capernaum that day to save two women.

A number of medical conditions could have been to blame. Maybe she was a hemophiliac, whose body was unable to form blood clots. Or she dealt with stomach ulcers, leaving her weakened and in constant abdominal pain. Her bleeding could have been connected with her menstrual cycle, making her unclean in the eyes of society. Or, for all we know, the woman could have been plagued with a chronic nosebleed.

Whatever the cause, she was hurting, cast off by the people around her, and desperate for a miracle.

If you've ever endured any kind of prolonged illness, you know how exhausting it can be. When this woman entered the crowd, she'd tried everything under the sun to find relief.

She'd attempted every form of treatment and medication prescribed to her. She may have even tried some wacky pre-Pinterest home remedies from the Talmud, the collection of Jewish oral traditions followed by people of faith.

The Talmud proposed eleven treatments to stop a woman's bleeding, and they were quirky to say the least. Some of the treatments involved the ashes of ostrich eggs, boiled onions, and some less than luscious wine. But they didn't work for her.

Chronic illnesses take their toll in more ways than one, and Scripture tells us she was bankrupt. Even if there were a groundbreaking new treatment that might cure her, she wouldn't have the financial means to access it.

In addition to being debilitated and bankrupt, she lived in isolation. To fully grasp the total desolation of her illness, you have to understand the significance of blood, specifically a woman bleeding, in Jewish culture.

Consider Leviticus 15:25, and you'll begin to understand what you need to know about her twelve-year battle: "If a woman has a flow of blood for many days that is unrelated to her menstrual period, or if the blood continues beyond the normal period, she is ceremonially unclean. As during her menstrual period, the woman will be unclean as long as the discharge continues" (NLT).

So she had been unclean for twelve years, and anyone who came into contact with her or with anything she touched would also be made unclean. She had to stay outside of the community while bleeding, and she couldn't enter the synagogue to worship for a week after she stopped. But she never stopped bleeding.

She could never go to the synagogue or the temple. She could never touch someone without making them unclean.

Imagine the implications. When people saw her coming, they probably ducked into a room or crossed the street just to avoid being close to her. Imagine trying to get married, have children, and play an active role in a community that considered you impure because of your medical condition.

Her sickness left her isolated from the people around her. It's conceivable that she had not known human touch for twelve years.

Now imagine the effect of her condition on her faith.

If this woman prayed once a day, every day, for God to heal her, that's 4,380 prayers over twelve years. What if she asked God for healing five times a day? That's 21,900 seemingly unanswered prayers. How might she have felt about herself with radio silence from God? How might she have thought God felt about her? Maybe he didn't want to touch her, either.

> If this woman prayed once a day, every day, for God to heal her, that's 4,380 prayers over twelve years. What if she asked God for healing five times a day? That's 21,900 seemingly unanswered prayers.

Yet this frail woman dragged her anemic body out of the house to fight her way to Jesus, hoping he could help her. The story of her encounter with him is brief, but the few verses we're given in Matthew 9, Mark 5, and Luke 8 tell us everything about the character of Christ and the sheer power of not giving up.

When there's no relief, no hope on the horizon, no prospect of healing, and no human solution, Jesus changes everything. He can do that for you. Have you given up? Then get back up. Have you stopped praying? Start praying again. Have you waited for years for a touch from God? Don't give up now, when you may be days or even moments away from an encounter with Jesus that will change everything.

A Desperate Reach

Mark 5:27–29 tells us, "When she heard about Jesus, she came up behind him in the crowd and touched his cloak, because she thought, 'If I just touch his clothes, I will be healed.' Immediately her bleeding stopped and she felt in her body that she was freed from her suffering."

Don't you love it when Scripture dials us in to someone's thought process?

When she heard about Jesus, she came. *Penniless, isolated, weak, and unclean, she came.*

After all the medical consultations in the world had failed her, she determined to fight her way to the only appointment that could make a difference. Jesus did more for her in a split second than every doctor in Israel could do for her in a lifetime.

But there's more significance to this divine appointment than what we see on the surface.

When she touched Jesus, "Immediately her bleeding stopped and she felt in her body that she was freed from her suffering. At once Jesus realized that power had gone out from him. He turned around in the crowd and asked, 'Who touched my clothes?'" (vv. 29–30).

His disciples are naturally perplexed by his question, quipping, "You see the people crowding against you . . . and yet you can ask, 'Who touched me?'" (v. 31).

What does he mean, who touched him? Um, everyone within three feet of us right now? Not following . . .

"Then the woman, knowing what had happened to her, came and fell at his feet and, trembling with fear, told him the whole truth" (v. 33).

The woman forbidden by the law from coming into God's presence for over a decade had reached out and grabbed God, and now she was standing face-to-face with God in the flesh.

A simple touch from Jesus has an immediate impact on us. He is powerful, for sure. But don't miss the fact that he's also accessible. You have access to Jesus. He doesn't isolate himself from you because you're sinful or unclean. On the contrary, he wants you to pursue him, to reach out for a touch from him, and to come directly to him when you have a need that only he can meet.

Jesus Changes Everything

By the letter of the law, touching a bleeding woman would have made Jesus unclean, but the opposite happened.

She didn't make Jesus dirty. He made her pure.

Rather than rebuking her, Jesus looked tenderly at the trembling woman who had just bared her soul to him and replied, "Daughter, your faith has healed you" (v. 34).

Did you catch that? First he called her daughter. How sweet this must have sounded to her. She hadn't heard anyone refer to her affectionately in a long, long time.

He continued with a beautiful blessing: "Go in peace and be freed from your suffering" (v. 34).

There's an abundance of hope wrapped in that sweet statement.

Jesus knew the turmoil and suffering she'd experienced: the anxiety, fear, and depression. He also knew the desperate faith it had taken her to fight through a mob of people to reach out and grab him. He knew her heart. And he breathed freedom and peace into her new life.

Yes in Christ

Jesus fulfills prophecy, but he also fulfills promises.

I love the way 2 Corinthians 1:20 describes this concept. In that passage, Scripture tells us, "For no matter how many promises God has made, they are 'Yes' in Christ."

The thousands of prayers this woman uttered weren't ignored. Every prayer, every desperate plea to God, and every tear she cried were answered in Christ.

She was healed physically and restored spiritually. There was so much more to her healing than a doctor could ever have provided.

Never again would she doubt if God valued her. Jesus healed her heart, not just her body.

God was working every single detail in her life to lead her to the streets of Capernaum that day, straight into his path. Her circumstances brought her to Jesus. Her faith healed her.

Banned from the temple, shunned from physical contact with anyone, she was now called *daughter* by God himself. In that instant, she was loved, cherished, and known by the only One whose opinion mattered.

Let's take it a step further. Jesus stopped what he was doing to heal her, and what he had been doing was of the utmost importance. The disciples had to wonder why Jesus halted his trek to Jairus's home. I'm sure Jairus was a nervous wreck: his daughter was literally on the verge of death.

You know what? Jesus didn't consider one daughter to be more worth his time than the other, or that one was religious royalty and the other was a bankrupt, bleeding woman.

He left this scene and went to Jairus's home. The people were mourning because the twelve-year-old girl died while Jesus was delayed. But as he was known to do, Jesus messed up their mourning—and raised her from the dead.

Yesterday and Today and Forever

Do you realize that Jesus offers that same compassion today?

Hebrews 13:8 says, "Jesus Christ is the same yesterday and today and forever." That's a promise you can bank on as surely as the bleeding woman banked on Malachi 4:2, which says, "But for you who fear my name, the Sun of Righteousness will rise with healing in his wings" (NLT). The Hebrew word we translate "wings," *kanaph*, was the same word used for the corners of the outer garment Jesus wore, the same garment she reached up and grabbed. *Kanaph* and *tzit tzit* referred to the edges of a garment where tassels hung as a reminder to Israel to obey God's commands (Num. 15:40; Deut. 22:12). So with the promise of Malachi 4:2 in mind, she saw Jesus as the Sun of Righteousness who came with healing in his wings (tassels) that day. She grabbed the edge of his cloak, his tassel, to find healing in his wings. Where doctors failed her, Jesus healed her.

You don't have to push through a horde of people to reach him. He's accessible. He may answer you instantly, or it may take years for his plan to come together. But he sees you, and he won't turn you away.

He knows your need, and he's closer than your next breath. How? Because the Son, with healing in his wings, has risen from the grave.

It doesn't matter if you're bleeding, depressed, or unclean. Because at the heart of every human being is an illness we can't cure, no matter how many sacrifices we make or rules we follow.

Are you ailing physically, mentally, or financially? Are you weak, broken, and defeated? Maybe you've lost hope that your situation will ever improve. Or perhaps you've been judged by the people around you, condemned by your brothers and sisters in Christ because of your past. Maybe you haven't met Jesus to begin with.

You don't have to push through a horde of people to reach him. He's accessible. He may answer you instantly, or it may take years for his plan to come together.

Wherever you are, know this: Jesus will fight through anything to get to you. No matter your past or present circumstances, he wants to transform your future. Reach out and grab hold of Jesus, because his presence is the thing that heals us from sickness, rescues us from sin, and raises us from the dead.

SEVEN

A Heart's Humble Prayer

My friend Grant will always have a special place in my heart for two reasons. First, when my kids were very young he always took time to notice them (who were at times obnoxious). He would kneel down to their level and speak to them with kindness, calling them by name, and they loved the attention they got from this college student.

The other reason I love Grant? He created my Twitter account in 2007.

I was debating with some of our staff about how social media was a stupid idea, and Twitter sounded too much like a small bird to be any good. While we argued, Grant grabbed my Blackberry (google it if you don't know what those were) and quietly set up my account.

While I was working on this book, I shared the concept behind it with a friend of mine. He told me that I needed to call Grant and find out what had happened to his grandfather.

Grant is part of a churchgoing family, but even though most of them are Christians, they never talked openly about salvation or their faith. But among all of his family members, there was one man whom he knew was not a follower of Jesus, his grandfather. Grant had grown up fearful that Papa Reeves would die and go to hell because he refused to become a Christian.

He was also afraid to ever say anything to his grandpa, because the two of them were very close. Papa Reeves was a lifelong Pepsi delivery man who loved Elvis Presley. He was also a Korean War vet who loved Grant with all of his heart. As he was eighty-three, Grant had concluded that it was too late for his papa. His heart was too hard.

In October 2018, our church was in a preaching series called "Testify," and we challenged people to be bold with their faith by sharing their salvation stories with people they loved. Grant, who had a brand-new baby at home, was convicted that he needed to finally take the risk and tell Papa how to be saved, and he drove to his grandfather's home. He was scared but hopeful. Eighty-three-year-old men do not usually convert to faith in Christ.

What made this situation even more urgent was that his grandfather was dying of throat cancer. The end was near, and the doctors had called in the family to say their goodbyes as hospice care began. Papa Reeves was about to die, and then he would stand before God and enter into eternity, most likely separated from God.

After an anxious drive and lots of prayer, Grant arrived at his papa's and asked the rest of the family to leave the room so that he could talk to him alone.

When he asked Papa Reeves if he was a Christian, he responded, "No I'm not. It's too late for me. I have to pay for all the sins I've committed."

Grant then told him how much God loved him, and how Jesus died to take away his sin and was raised from the dead to forgive him and give him a new life. Then Grant simply asked him if wanted to be reborn.

To his amazement, his grandpa said yes. He simply didn't know how.

With a heart about to burst, Grant prayed with his grandfather. He asked him to pray out loud too, asking Jesus to come into his heart and make him a new person. Through labored words, at times barely audible from the ravages of throat cancer, Dennis Reeves put his faith in Jesus.

His Best Week Was His Last Week

"He was able to say 'Come into my life,' and 'I give my life to you,' out loud, and it was one of the most amazing moments of my life," Grant said. "So we cried and talked about the Lord, and I gave him my Bible that I used during college—one that I had with me every summer at Crossroads while working for you.

"For the next several days, my family said that he didn't put his Bible down. He slept with it and read it as much as he possibly could before he declined."

Dennis Reeves, eighty-three years old, was reborn on October 7.

On October 10 they took him to hospice, and he died on October 12.

Those final five days were the best days of his life. His own wife testified to this. "My grandmother and my dad both say to this day that the best week of Papa's life was the last week, because you could tell something was different and that he had a relationship with Jesus," Grant said.

This is the definition of cutting it close, right? And yet the miracle of God's grace is that he pursued Papa Reeves for over eight decades, up and down the roads of Anderson, South Carolina, delivering crates of Pepsi, all the way to Asia as he fought in the Korean War, and right up to the moment that hospice came in to help him meet the inevitable end of his life.

Dennis Reeves, eighty-three years old, was reborn on October 7. On October 10 they took him to hospice, and he died on October 12. Those final five days were the best days of his life.

And as he approached death, Jesus was right there. Beside him. Giving him a chance to be changed. Dennis Reeves encountered Jesus five days before he died. It certainly changed everything for him—because it changed where he would spend eternity.

As we keep looking at how Jesus interacted with people, two things are evident.

First, he loves saving, healing, and rescuing people. Second, he does it simply because he loves them. No one deserves it. Salvation can't be achieved. It can only be received. It's a gift, and we have to simply take it and say thank you.

To be reborn, we have to receive.

Between Two Thieves

As it turns out, Papa Reeves wasn't the first dying man whom Jesus was right beside as he prepared to breathe his last breath.

Five days before Jesus went to the cross, the streets of Jerusalem were lined with his adoring fans and followers, who laid palm branches at his feet to create a pathway for him as a display of honor. Many people believed him to be the Messiah who would rescue Israel from Rome's occupation. Others believed he was the Son of God, with a supernatural reign that transcended politics altogether. The people cried out, "Hosanna! Blessed is he who comes in the name of the Lord!" (Mark 11:9).

He fulfilled Zechariah 9:9, which predicted that the king would ride humbly into the city on a donkey.

But just a few days later, many of those same people were crying out for his crucifixion in exchange for the release of a murderer. That Friday, they stood at the foot of Golgotha, the hillside named, literally, "the skull," spitting vitriol at him as he drew in his last ragged breaths on a convicted criminal's cross.

There he hung, between two criminals convicted for the acts they had committed. It was only fitting that Jesus spent his last moments surrounded by sinners. That's who he came for, even earning the reputation as a "friend of sinners." Rather than isolating himself from the broken, he was drawn to them and was known for dining with tax collectors, prostitutes, and outcasts.

While the religious leaders were too self-righteous to touch sinners, Jesus was too consumed with his mission not to. Jesus lived his whole life among broken and lost people, loving them too fiercely to abandon them, and that's where he died, guided by that same mission.

Every word Jesus spoke on the cross that dreadful day radiated compassion and forgiveness, even toward the ones who were crucifying him. As Jesus looked out on the crowd of people relishing in his torment, while nearing suffocation, he felt no malice or contempt.

Instead of heaping curses on the people who put him to death, he prayed blessings upon them.

"Father, forgive them, for they do not know what they are doing," he cried out (Luke 23:34). With spikes driven through his wrists and ankles, in a world of pain we cannot even imagine, he prayed for the very men who'd used a sledgehammer to drive the spikes through his flesh.

Jesus literally prayed for the forgiveness of his murderers while they were murdering him. Let that sink in.

His heart was also tuned to the men suffering on either side of him.

In most translations and traditional tellings, the men hanging on either side of Jesus are simply referred to as thieves or criminals. The word used to describe the men, *lēstai* in Matthew and *lēstas* in Mark, could have multiple meanings but usually referred to violent robbers and thieves. Another possible interpretation of the word is more closely related to rebels or revolutionaries. Either way, these men weren't pacifists following Jesus from village to village. They were outlaws, the same type of criminal as Barabbas, the man freed in exchange for Jesus's life.

Jesus literally prayed for the forgiveness of his murderers while they were murdering him. Let that sink in.

In Jesus's time, crucifixions were primarily inflicted upon lower-class citizens, slaves, and servants, and rarely targeted the upper class or Roman citizens. The crimes punishable by crucifixion could range anywhere from stealing to murder, with a whole host of acts in between, such as political insurrection.

The environment at Golgotha was hostile, with a crowd of spectators hurling insults at him. As Jesus prayed for their forgiveness, the people taunted, "He saved others; let him save himself if he is God's Messiah, the Chosen One" (v. 35).

Luke tells us the soldiers standing at his feet joined in. "If you are the king of the Jews," they sneered, "save yourself" (v. 37).

Adding insult to injury, one of the criminals enduring the same brutal crucifixion joined in on the taunting. "Aren't you the Messiah?" he asked. "Save yourself and us!" (v. 39).

Some people, like this dying man, for numerous reasons, choose to rebel against God, to deny his existence, to mock anyone who follows Jesus, and to shame and ridicule people of faith. Jesus loves each of them, and the Holy Spirit in you can give you the grace to love them too.

Jesus Never Stops Saving

While the criminal to his left spewed bitter vitriol at Jesus, laughing at the notion of him being the Messiah, the man hanging to his right knew better and rebuked the other criminal.

Jesus's death on the cross was laced with symbolism, right down to his placement between the two criminals and the postures they assumed.

Matthew 25:31–34 lets us in on what's to come for humanity on the day of judgment, using the symbolism of sheep and goats:

> When the Son of Man comes in his glory, and all the angels with him, he will sit on his glorious throne. All the nations will be gathered before him, and he will separate the people one from another as a shepherd separates the sheep from the goats. He will put the *sheep on his right* and the *goats on his left*. Then the King will say to those on his right, "Come, you who are blessed by my Father; take your inheritance, the kingdom prepared for you since the creation of the world."

There's a reason Scripture describes people as goats and sheep. If you've spent any time on a farm and been around goats, this classification makes sense. Goats are stubborn and proud, constantly trying to elevate and assert themselves. That's why the goat is the symbol of Satanism, epitomizing the goals and character of Satan and his followers. They have to ascend. They're always climbing. They have to have the highest place. They fight each other for dominance.

Stay low instead of trying to climb high. It takes humility to admit we need to be reborn, but that's the path to salvation.

Sheep, on the other hand, are helpless, innocent animals needing leadership and fostering. Time and time again, the Bible describes Jesus as the Shepherd who guides and protects the sheep from their own devices, leaving behind the ninety-nine to chase after the one who has gone astray. So Jesus hung on the middle cross that day with a haughty, proud mocker on his left and a humble man on his right, a perfect picture of the dividing line between the sheep on the right and the goats on the left.

We should aspire to be more like sheep and less like goats. Strive for humility. Stop asserting ourselves and start abiding in God's love. Stay low instead of trying to climb high. It takes humility to admit we need to be reborn, but that's the path to salvation.

A Broken Prayer

As the criminal on the left mocked Jesus with bitterness and resentment, the thief to his right responded in humility.

"'Don't you fear God,' he said, 'since you are under the same sentence? We are punished justly, for we are getting what our deeds deserve. But this man has done nothing wrong'" (Luke 23:40).

In the middle of a painful, public death, this man knew where he stood. He was aware of his own sin and the sinlessness of the Man hanging beside him, and he was aching for redemption.

So, at the punishing block of bandits, rebels, and murderers, the blameless Son of God fought through his beleaguered breaths to have a conversation with an undeserving convict.

His lungs filling with blood and his legs moments away from being broken, the thief knew there was no escaping death. He realized how little life he had left, wrestling with the fact that soon he would be standing before God and his judgment.

He was convicted of a crime bad enough to warrant a public execution, one that he owned up to committing. He didn't hide his sin. He didn't excuse it. He didn't blame someone else or blame the system. He confessed his guilt and owned the punishment.

This man was faced with the same sobering reality all of us are: as soon as we close our eyes to this life, we will open them to eternity.

Racked with guilt, he came to Jesus with one broken and humble plea. "Remember me when you come into your kingdom" (v. 42).

His request was simple but it held tremendous power. He had just professed Jesus as Lord, proclaiming his authority to forgive sins and overcome death.

The Roman government wasn't the only body that convicted the thief on the cross that day. He was under the conviction of the Holy Spirit, who compelled him to seek Jesus's forgiveness. That's the same conviction each of us feels before we're reborn. Then, once we meet Jesus, we feel that same conviction when we sin or drift away from Christ. It's the Holy Spirit drawing us back to Jesus.

That thief could've gone to his grave declaring his innocence, cast the blame on other people, or died with a hardened heart. Instead, he repented. With nothing to lose and no one to impress, he confessed his sin, loudly and publicly, and sought the mercy of God.

Rather than standing before God, he was hanging beside him.

"Remember me," was his heart's humble prayer. And what a beautiful prayer this is, the kind uttered in complete, heartfelt desperation, knowing it is too late to atone for past sins. Mercy is the only hope.

Just think of me. Don't forget me.

Jesus saw a broken spirit and a contrite heart in the prayer of this convict who deserved nothing but his wrath and judgment.

Like the man beside him, Jesus was also in the final heartbeats of his life, so his response to the contrite criminal was short and to the point, and like the prayer before it, was equally beautiful in its simplicity.

"Truly I tell you, today you will be with me in paradise," Jesus answered him, putting his guilt-ridden mind at ease (v. 43).

It was this man's sin that had put Jesus on the cross, but as grievous as sin is in the presence of our holy God, he didn't want to punish him, nor does he want to punish us today. Instead, he made a way to pardon us, bearing the burden and paying the penalty himself.

"Truly I tell you" are the words used in the NIV and several other translations; other versions translate Jesus's words here as, "I tell you the truth," or "I assure you."

In other words, Jesus didn't leave him wondering whether or not he was forgiven. On the contrary, he assured the man that he would indeed remember his confession of sin and profession of faith, then promised him that they would be in paradise together the moment he breathed his last.

Can you imagine the relief that washed over his heavy heart in that moment? That's the kind of peace that floods our hearts when we're reborn, when we confess our sin and receive his grace, when we pray, when we worship, when we fellowship with sisters and brothers.

The Son of God granted him a miraculous pardon. This is the only way any of us will make it to heaven. Our sins will be punished or they will be pardoned.

Four Simple Steps to Salvation

You and I are saved the same way the dying thief was saved.

1. He was convicted. Truth be told, he was double-convicted. Found guilty of breaking Roman law, he was convicted of a crime punishable by death. But there was a heavier weight that rested on his shoulders—the knowledge that he deserved to die because he was guilty. No excuses. No deflecting. No blaming. This is the posture we must take when we come to Jesus.

2. He confessed. With his own mouth he declared that he was getting what he deserved. The crowd heard it. The other criminal heard it. Jesus heard it. But this was not an apology. It was repentance. Then he followed his confession with a humble request: "Remember me when you come into your kingdom" (v. 42). It's only through confession of sin that we turn to Jesus for pardon of sin and assurance of salvation.

3. He converted. He was fully convinced that his only hope was Jesus. He indicated his faith in Christ when he said, "Remember me when you come into *your* kingdom." He acknowledged that once they died, Jesus alone would have authority in the afterlife.

4. He had confidence. He did, after all, die. But he died clutching a promise he'd been given by Jesus. After an apparent life of regret with no accomplishments or achievements to show for his years on earth, how amazing that he could die with confidence in the simple, gentle words spoken to him by his new friend who was dying beside him! We can live with this same confidence and can die one day knowing that we are secure in the hands of God.

Nothing to Offer

The thief couldn't pay off his debt or work off his guilt. He was literally hanging on for dear life, with nothing to offer but his humble heart and a desperate plea for grace.

Do you realize we're in the same boat? We may not be murderous bandits on death row, but we've sinned plenty of times, and that's enough to make us guilty. But that isn't bad news, because the reality is, if God's loving grace was based on our performance, none of us would experience it.

The stunning thing about being reborn is that God loves us because he is God, not because we are good. Our value and identity come from being made by God and loved by God.

It all boils down to this: you could never do anything so bad that it would keep you out of the kingdom of God, and you could never do anything so good that you could get yourself there on your own.

Salvation comes through one action and one alone: the perfect sacrifice of the sinless Son of God, two thousand years ago on a tree at Calvary, hanging beside a forgiven sinner.

When Jesus spoke new life into this man, he spoke a new identity over him. No longer was he a guilty thief but a beloved child of God, just like that.

Because of Jesus's compassion, he was able to die with confidence, because the Messiah of the world had just made him a promise he could stand upon.

Can you imagine that thief, laboring and struggling fiercely just to catch a breath, barely holding on to consciousness, until he couldn't bear it any longer? Then, in an instant, the pain had ceased, the nails were gone, and he felt nothing but peace. I can't help but think the very first thing he saw when the lights came on in the kingdom of God was that same loving face he had just locked eyes with for the last time on earth, as Jesus extended a nail-scarred hand and invited him in.

The stunning thing about being reborn is that God loves us because he is God, not because we are good. Our value and identity come from being made by God and loved by God.

He's still reaching out to guilty sinners. I can see him with his arms stretched out to the left and the right, with rusty metal spikes driven through his wrists, as his crucified hands reached further, to the criminals on his right and his left, bidding them to come to him for salvation.

He died with his arms open to sinners. It's the way he lived, and it's still his posture today—welcoming, bidding, calling, asking anyone and everyone to repent of their sin and join his family. Offering a place in paradise.

Whether you are in the prime of your life or on your death-bed like the thief on the cross or Papa Reeves, you are loved by a God who was hammered onto a tree so you could be reborn.

You can't achieve it. Just receive it.

EIGHT
Wasted Opportunity

When I think back on my childhood, my mind is flooded with snapshots of people, places, and things that left indelible marks on my memory. I remember watching *Looney Tunes* and *Scooby-Doo* on Saturday mornings, which was the only day cartoons were on TV back in the 1970s. I recall hearing Bob Seger, the Pointer Sisters, and Van Halen on the radio as my mom drove me to elementary school in her Chevy station wagon. I remember buying "Thriller" by Michael Jackson and "Purple Rain" by Prince on vinyl and listening to them on a record player in my room. (Record players like mine can now be found in the Smithsonian Museum, ancient history section.)

And I remember going to the Greenville Memorial Auditorium on Monday nights with my dad and other boys from my Sunday school class to watch professional wrestling.

I know, I know. I can see you roll your eyes. I am not defending or condoning it. I just need you to know that in the region of the country where I grew up, from the 1970s to the early 2000s, pro wrestling was a cultural phenomenon on the same level as NASCAR and sweet tea.

The sad reality now is the untimely demise of many of those men who were superstars in the strange subculture that grew to become a billion-dollar industry. Much has been written about wrestlers who died prematurely: Randy "The Macho Man" Savage, The Ultimate Warrior, Rowdy Roddy Piper, Eddie Guerrero, Ravishing Rick Rude, The British Bulldog, and many more.

Entire families were affected by this horrible trend. Kerry Von Erich, a second-generation wrestler from Texas, took the wrestling world by storm. He became a world champion and sold out arenas. Tragically, at the age of thirty-three he committed suicide by shooting himself in the heart. Two of his brothers, both professional wrestlers, also took their own lives.

It's unsettling to read the stories of people who worked so hard to rise to the pinnacle of success in their profession only to see the very thing they so desperately wanted lead to their death. In many of these cases, the bodies they spent so many years sculpting for the large crowds they entertained were riddled with injuries and chronic pain. Drug and alcohol abuse was a common denominator in many of their deaths. So was depression.

But no story is as heartbreaking as the story of Chris Benoit. He was called "The Canadian Crippler" for a reason. Widely considered the toughest man to ever enter a wrestling ring, he's respected as the best fighter, pound for pound, to ever hold the World Championship. He dismantled opponents. He trained relentlessly, beginning at age fourteen. He put his body through unbelievable abuse, attempting moves that no one else would even dream of.

His signature move was a diving headbutt. He would climb to the top of a ten-foot-tall steel cage, pause, then launch his body forward like a missile, leading with his head, and landing on the hard mat below as his head concussed off his opponent. There's speculation that the repeated trauma to his head injured his brain, causing Chronic Traumatic Encephalopathy, or CTE, and all the side effects of that disease.

In 2007, in his home in Georgia, Chris Benoit did the unthinkable. According to ABC News,

> On June 25, 2007, an unimaginable horror was discovered inside of Chris Benoit's home in Fayetteville, Ga., when police stopped by on a "welfare check" after Benoit had missed several appointments, according to the *Atlanta Journal-Constitution*.
>
> Officers found his wife Nancy strangled to death and their 7-year-old son Daniel appeared to have been suffocated. Bibles were found next to their bodies. Benoit's body was found hanging from a weight machine in the basement.
>
> "We're ruling it as a double homicide-suicide," said Fayette County Sheriff's Lt. Tommy Pope.*

My heart breaks when I think about all that he had access to, all the success, the loving family, the fame, and the money . . . and it all vanished in an unexplainable act of destruction.

What makes this story so gut-wrenching for me is the fact that I met Chris Benoit not long before he killed his family and then himself. We actually spent several minutes face-to-face, just a few feet from each other.

*Ethan Nelson and Roxanna Sherwood, "Chris Benoit's Murder, Suicide: Was Brain Damage to Blame?" ABC News, August 26, 2010, https://abcnews.go .com/Nightline/chris-benoits-dad-son-suffered-severe-brain-damage/story?id =11471875.

A Wasted Opportunity

I was returning home from a speaking engagement and had a layover in Atlanta. I was on an escalator when I noticed the guy standing next to me. He was significantly shorter than I thought he'd be, but I immediately knew who he was. Starstruck, I held up four fingers without saying a word. He smiled and flashed back four fingers to me, a symbol of The Four Horsemen, which was the clique of wrestlers he ran with in his story line on TV. He could tell I was a fan, so we started chatting about the latest feud, his upcoming matches, and how busy his travel schedule was.

We rode that long escalator all the way to the top of the terminal and stepped off together. We talked for an additional five minutes, then I shook his hand and told him what an honor it was to meet him. He was truly gracious. He engaged me in conversation like an old friend. He didn't act like a superstar. Nothing indicated that he was fighting a battle that would soon be the end of him and his family.

As I shook his hand, I sensed a strong desire to share the gospel with him. I had an opportunity to tell Chris Benoit how Jesus had changed everything for me. It was clear. I needed to tell him how Jesus had saved me. Nothing was stopping me. He was right there.

Instead, I chickened out.

I never said a word to him about Jesus. As he walked away, I immediately regretted it. Then I justified it by telling myself that he was in a hurry. Or that I didn't want to rush through it and make him feel like it was a sales pitch. Or that there were hundreds of people pushing past us in the Atlanta airport, and it wasn't the appropriate place to bring up something so eternally important.

Then, just months later, I heard the news. Major networks were reporting it. ESPN was talking about it. Speculation was swirling about possible CTE, roid rage, drug abuse, prescription painkillers, and a major psychotic break.

And all I could think about was standing there in the airport, shaking his hand, having the urge to tell him how Jesus could change his life, and then walking away without saying a word.

Would it have changed my level of urgency if I had known Chris Benoit would commit suicide at age forty? You'd better believe it.

Judas, the Opportunist

Not everyone who hears the gospel is actually changed by it in a positive way. Some people choose to reject God's love. The same was true when Jesus walked the earth. Not everyone yielded to his demands that they repent of their sins, deny themselves, take up their cross, and become his disciple. One of his own handpicked disciples proves this point.

I'm talking about Judas Iscariot.

We know him as a traitor who turned Jesus over to the Jewish powers and the Roman guards. He did it for money, a measly thirty pieces of silver. And to add insult to injury, he identified Jesus to the soldiers in the darkness of the garden of Gethsemane with a kiss. An act of affection shared between friends and family members was hijacked by a power-grabbing opportunist willing to sell out his friend for the equivalent of less than two hundred dollars.

Not everyone who hears the gospel is actually changed by it in a positive way. Some people choose to reject God's love.

Did Judas betray Jesus for the money? Was it really about a side hustle to make a little extra cash? Probably. John tells us that Judas was a thief, and he would have known because he spent over three years with him. According to his eyewitness account, John reveals that Judas had a history of working all the angles to pad the account with more cash so he could take a personal cut when no one was looking.

When Mary, the sister of Lazarus, went to extravagant lengths to shower Jesus with expensive perfume, Judas decried a wasted opportunity. John saw the real Judas and added his own commentary to the story.

> But one of his disciples, Judas Iscariot, who was later to betray him, objected, "Why wasn't this perfume sold and the money given to the poor? It was worth a year's wages." He did not say this because he cared about the poor but because he was a thief; as keeper of the money bag, he used to help himself to what was put into it. (John 12:4–6)

Was Judas also motivated by jealousy toward the rest of the disciples, most of whom were from the northern region of Israel? Peter, Andrew, James, and John (just to name two sets of brothers) were from Galilee. Judas, however, was from the south of Israel, and the rivalry went deep into Jewish history, reaching back to the northern and southern kingdoms of David's reign. Perhaps he saw himself as a shrewd and educated Jew of higher class and better fabric than the roughneck Galileans with thick accents and questionable stock. He could've had something to prove; namely, that he was better than them. Smarter than them. And ultimately, more powerful than them.

Did Judas betray Jesus to force him into a showdown with the authorities? This is a popular theory, and one that I

WASTED OPPORTUNITY   133

personally lean toward. If Judas was lusting after power, then Jesus was the vehicle to get him there. And what better time to force his hand than during the Passover, when Jerusalem was bursting at the seams with Jews from all over the region, each despising the corrupt religious leaders of the temple and the pagan invaders, the Roman occupiers?

He'd seen Jesus control nature, cast out demons, and summon a dead man from a tomb. Jesus had real power. Judas wasn't looking for a suffering servant or a spiritual Savior. He was looking for a military coup, a fire-breathing avenger, a messiah thirsty for blood and vengeance.

He wanted a king who would crush all enemies, specifically the Romans who had invaded Israel and taxed the Jews into poverty. In Jesus's new empire, Judas could be the Chief of Staff. Or Secretary of the Treasury.

Simply put, Judas grew tired of waiting on Jesus, so he devised a plan to force Jesus to act. He would betray him and turn him over to the Jewish religious elite who hated him and wanted him dead. When they attempted to arrest him, Jesus would retaliate, once and for all unleashing his real power. The revolution would begin, and Judas would be right beside Jesus to see the whole thing go down.

The sooner Jesus dispatched his powers on his opponents, the quicker Judas could sit at his right hand, creating an empire and telling people what to do. There would be no limit to his influence or the amount of money he could make. Or take.

From the moment he kissed Christ in Gethsemane, events were set in motion that could not be stopped. They would lead to the death of Jesus and the suicide of Judas.

Terrible things happen when we reject Jesus. Saying no to his offer of salvation leads to a life without purpose or peace and an eternity without hope. But even after we've been reborn, we may find ourselves subtly saying no to his promptings, his conviction of sin, and the nudging of the Holy Spirit. Even as Christians, we have to fight the urge to drift back into old ways of thinking.

A Previous Wasted Opportunity

Judas's story plays out like a Greek tragedy. Jesus does the exact opposite of what Judas had planned. Instead of vaporizing his opponents in a holy rage, Jesus lays down his life as a sacrifice. Judas realizes the mistake he made and, in a fit of superstition, he tries to give the thirty pieces of silver back to the corrupt religious officials he had colluded with. The details of his remorse and his reaction of throwing the money back into the temple from where it came look almost identical to an Old Testament story—or as we might call it, the backstory.

Hundreds of years earlier, the prophet Zechariah spoke a word to Israel about the annulment of a covenant God had made with his people. As was customary then, prophets earned a wage that was equivalent to the authority they carried and with which they spoke. When Zechariah delivered God's message to the people, he asked for payment and was given thirty pieces of silver. He threw it right back at them (Zech. 11:12–13).

Why did Zechariah throw it back into the temple? Because the amount of money was not just embarrassingly low to pay a prophet, it was also layered with deep meaning. It was the exact value of a slave, dating back to the book of Exodus.

Symbolically, they were saying that Zechariah had no more value to them than a slave. He came as a prophet and spoke the Word of God to them. In return they dishonored him by ascribing to him a very low value.

When Judas betrayed Jesus for the same amount, it communicates that Judas never valued Jesus. Jesus was just a means to an end. He could easily sell Jesus like a slave owner sold a slave. So when Judas saw that he wouldn't get what he really wanted, he got rid of the blood money by doing the exact same thing Zechariah had done 450 years earlier.

Remorse isn't the same thing as repentance. Remorse is being sorry you got caught. Repentance is feeling sorrow at the level of your heart's motivation and doing something about it.

Judas felt remorse. But it did not lead him to repentance. He was heartbroken, but not for the right reason. He was suicidal because his plan failed. An innocent man had been killed and the blood was on his hands.

> Remorse isn't the same thing as repentance. Remorse is being sorry you got caught. Repentance is feeling sorrow at the level of your heart's motivation and doing something about it.

He had just known for sure that Jesus would rise up to defend himself. Instead, Jesus stood silent while his accusers lied about him and illegally condemned him to death. Had Judas been hiding in the shadows during the trial that night? I think so. His plan had been carefully crafted, and he wanted to see it through. It would play out.

Except it didn't. He watched his life's ambition vaporize before him. There would be no place of power for him. Judas lost his bet. He got rid of the minuscule amount of money as soon as he could. But it didn't help, and it didn't matter. He didn't want a king who was willing to die. He wanted a king who would crush his enemies. But Jesus wasn't that kind of king. He wasn't building that kind of kingdom.

Judas wasn't paying attention when Jesus predicted his death and resurrection. He was too busy plotting his own plan to submit to God's. He could have repented but his grief led him to take his own life instead. And wasn't that his problem all along? His life had always been his own, when he should have given it to Jesus.

Beware of the subtle temptation of using Jesus as a way to get something else you want.

When we walk in the direction of blind ambition, it leads us to a destination of destruction. Beware of the subtle temptation of using Jesus as a way to get something else you want. That was the trap Judas fell into, and look where it took him.

A Last Chance to Be Reborn

Just hours before the betrayal, Jesus extended one final opportunity to Judas. It's found in a small detail recorded during Jesus's last meal with his disciples in John 13:26. It was the Feast of the Passover, which the Jews had celebrated since they fled Egypt during the days of Moses. This meal was layered with symbolism. For Judas, it was his last opportunity to be reborn.

Many of us have a mental image of "The Last Supper" based on the eponymous 1495 painting by Leonardo da Vinci in Milan, Italy. Factual and historical inaccuracies aside, this famous work of art brings us to a moment where it seems Jesus is extending one final act of grace to his betrayer.

Jesus personalized an act of friendship and forgiveness for Judas, an act so small and simple that Westerners like us glance right over it. When Jesus dips his hand into the cup, he's doing what they still do today in Israel. I've done it numerous times myself, dipping broken bread in olive oil and then eating it. Yet this time Jesus doesn't place the bread in his own mouth. He hands it to Judas. The meaning is clear to any Middle Easterner. Jesus is not only showing kindness to Judas. He's showing his love for him. It was customary for the host to offer a guest a morsel of bread as a gesture of love and friendship. So what Jesus did was not unusual, but because of the circumstances it was unusually significant.

This took place during the Passover feast. Jesus dipped the bread for the feast into the sauce for the paschal (Passover) lamb.

During the original Passover in Egypt, the Jews were instructed by God in Exodus 12 to dip a hyssop branch into a bowl filled with the blood of a sacrificial lamb and spread it over the doorpost of their homes so that the angel of death would "pass over" their families instead of taking the life of their firstborn son.

Thousands of years later, the perfect Lamb of God (and God's only Son) is about to spill his blood on the cross, but before he lays down his life, he dips bread, not hyssop, into a bowl filled with paschal oil, not blood. He offers it to Judas, not an actual angel of death but a human agent who will bring death to Jesus, the final sacrifice for all sin.

Judas is, in effect, the new death angel, and Jesus is the new lamb whose blood won't just cover up sin. It will wash it away. His blood won't cover an Egyptian doorpost; it will cover a Roman cross.

Jesus shows his love for Judas by extending an opportunity to repent of the evil scheme in his heart and be reconciled with

Jesus at the table. Judas does eat the bread, and symbolically, as it enters his mouth, pure evil enters his soul, and he sets out to put his plan in motion. He rejected Jesus, but he intended to use him for his own agenda.

There's one more detail worth mentioning. Jesus quotes or alludes to the Old Testament dozens of times in the Gospels. What book does he quote from most frequently? The book of Psalms. He quotes it directly as he hangs on the cross. He quotes it as he resists Satan's temptations in the wilderness. And as he shares his bread with Judas, Jesus is alluding to this verse: "Even my close friend, someone I trusted, one who shared my bread, has turned against me" (Ps. 41:9).

The story of Judas is a tragedy. It's the most epic of all epic fails. It's the definition of wasted opportunity. Judas could have been reborn, at the table, sitting beside Jesus. What a waste to be that close to the King of Kings and miss the eternal bliss of knowing Christ for the promise of a pathetic few years with earthly wealth and power. Ironically, Judas didn't even get that.

This is the story of humanity. It's my story and yours. We have our own ideas of who God is and what he should do for us. Unaware of our own selfishness, we create expectations and turn them into self-seeking prayers that we hurl toward heaven, not realizing we often try to use God as a way of getting what we want for ourselves. This is why we have to be reborn.

Our broken humanity seeks its own desires. The great mistake we make is in thinking that anything other than God will truly satisfy us. This was the tragedy of Judas. He had access to Jesus. Close, personal proximity. A front-row seat to the miraculous. Firsthand knowledge of his teachings. He encountered the Christ. But for Judas, it wasn't enough. It wasn't what he wanted. He didn't actually want Jesus. He wanted what Jesus could give him. Power. Control.

Judas didn't want heavenly virtue. He wanted earthly power. But he didn't live long enough to realize that it was too small a thing to satisfy his soul. He hung himself, presumably from a tree, when the one man who could save him was hung on a tree in his place.

He hung himself, presumably from a tree, when the one man who could save him was hung on a tree in his place.

According to Deuteronomy 21:23, anyone who hangs on a tree is cursed. Judas died under the curse that Jesus died to free him from. And that has to go down in history as the greatest wasted opportunity of all time.

One Last Opportunity

You may wonder if it was even possible for Judas to be reborn. I've asked the same question about people whom I've seen reject the free offer of salvation. The fact that one can reject grace is proof that they can also receive it.

What I couldn't get over, as I thought about my encounter with Chris Benoit, was the wasted opportunity to tell a man about Jesus just months before he would meet Jesus. I still feel remorse over it, but unlike Judas, I am not led to despair because of it. My remorse motivates me to boldness. To speak the name of Jesus and tell how he changed me and changes people.

They called Chris Benoit "The Crippler" because of how he dismantled his opponents. We call Judas "The Traitor" because he turned against Jesus and sold him out for money and power. But these nicknames don't nearly communicate the full scope of these men or their identities. I believe that Jesus simply calls them "Beloved."

How it must break the heart of Jesus to see a world full of beloved children, all bearing the image of God, wasting opportunities to be reborn.

NINE

So You Would Believe

Nothing drives me nuts faster than being forced to wait. When I can't get what I need quickly, a chain reaction of events begins inside my mind. I get hot. My blood pressure rises. I begin to configure scenarios in which I take control of the situation and bypass the line. Whether it's the DMV, the grocery store, or the TSA checkpoint at the airport, I would rather be mugged by Swiss Ninjas than wait on anything.

Unless I know there's a huge payoff at the end.

Jesus made some folks wait in John 11. It all happened so that people would believe.

It was a tear-filled day in the town of Bethany, about two miles from Jerusalem. Mary and Martha had just lost their brother, Lazarus. He became sick and died within a matter of days. Grieving his death, they were joined at home by a group of mourners.

The two sisters were teeming with emotions, one of which was heartbreak. They were devastated, leaning on each other and their loved ones for support as they said goodbye to their brother.

They also felt shock. Lazarus's illness had come on so quickly. In a moment, their world was turned upside down.

But they had an advantage. They were close friends with Jesus, the healer. They would call on him. He would come. But Lazarus was dead before he got there. And buried. This was the definition of discouragement.

The One Jesus Loved

The sisters felt a great sense of confusion.

They hosted Jesus in their home. He was like family. They knew him, they loved him, and they had desperately needed him a few days ago.

As soon as Lazarus fell ill, they immediately called on their friend. But in their greatest moment of need, when they had hoped for his intervention, Jesus didn't show up.

In fact, when his friends from Bethany came to deliver word of Lazarus's illness, Jesus stayed put for a couple of days, simply stating, "This sickness will not end in death. No, it is for God's glory so that God's Son may be glorified through it" (John 11:4).

And while they waited, Lazarus died.

Is He Asleep? Or Is He Dead?

When Jesus got the urgent message to come quickly to Bethany to heal Lazarus, he said, "Our friend Lazarus has fallen asleep; but I am going there to wake him up" (v. 11).

The disciples, completely unaware of Jesus's meaning, responded, "Lord, if he sleeps, he will get better" (v. 12). The reason he hadn't rushed to Bethany to heal Lazarus was because he knew Lazarus was already on the mend, right?

Jesus was, in fact, aware of Lazarus's current state. He had been all along. He broke down the reality of the situation, spelling it out plainly: "Lazarus is dead, and for your sake I am glad I was not there, *so that you may believe*" (vv. 14–15).

The disciples were crushed. Lazarus was dead. These men were headed to a funeral.

So why had Jesus waited two days?

Jesus was now leading his disciples into a doubly difficult predicament: a dead man's wake and a death trap of their own. An angry mob had tried to kill Jesus the last time he was in the region of Judea. They would be heading that direction now.

Jesus doesn't always lead us to safe places. He often walks with us into uncertain and terrifying situations to show us his power. For a miracle to take place, it must first be preceded by a situation that demands a miracle. We want the surprise of a resurrection and the celebration of answered prayer, but we'd rather dodge the situation that requires desperation. We complain about the hard times that drive us to our knees before God to seek his intervention. A miracle first requires a mess.

> *We complain about the hard times that drive us to our knees before God to seek his intervention. A miracle first requires a mess.*

We don't see the miracle until things get so bad that only a miracle can change the outcome.

Death and Belief in Bethany

By the time Jesus reached Bethany, Lazarus had been in the tomb four days.

Jesus cared deeply for Lazarus, so much so that when the messenger rushed from Bethany to deliver word of his condition, he simply told the Lord, "The one you love is sick" (v. 3).

If he loved him so much, why had he not intervened to heal Lazarus? He was mere miles away and he let Lazarus suffer and die.

Word of his arrival reached the house, and Martha ran to the path to meet Jesus. "Lord," she cried out, "if you had been here, my brother would not have died" (v. 21).

But there was faith mixed with her doubt. "But I know that even now God will give you whatever you ask," she said (v. 22).

Jesus breathed hope, prophesying the miracle that was about to occur: "Your brother will rise again" (v. 23). She answered, "I know he will rise again in the resurrection at the last day" (v. 24).

Martha thought Jesus meant eventually. Jesus meant immediately.

Jesus waited on purpose, because there is always a purpose behind God's plans. We don't see it when we want to, but God reveals it when he wants to.

Then Jesus uttered the words that made the impossible possible: "I am the resurrection and the life. The one who *believes in me* will live, even though they die; and whoever lives by *believing in me* will never die" (vv. 25–26).

Then he asked her a simple question. "Do you *believe* this?" (v. 26). While Martha might not have completely grasped the meaning of his words, she was certain of one thing, replying confidently: "Yes, Lord. . . . I *believe* that you are the Messiah, the Son of God, who is to come into the world" (v. 27).

It's clear that Jesus wanted them to believe in him, and he was about to give them a reason to do so.

So Jesus urged her to call for her sister Mary and come back to him. Scripture tells us, "When Mary heard this, she got up quickly and went to him. Now Jesus had not yet entered the village, but was still at the place where Martha had met him" (vv. 29–30). Consumed with grief and desperate for something—anything—from Jesus to help make sense of what had happened, Mary raced to meet him. When she reached Jesus, "she fell at his feet and cried out, 'Lord, if you had been here, my brother would not have died'" (v. 32).

John says, "When Jesus saw her weeping, and the Jews who had come along with her also weeping, he was deeply moved in spirit and troubled" (v. 33). Heavy with hurt and compassion for the mourning people around him, he asked the sisters where Lazarus was laid to rest.

As they led him to the tomb, Jesus did something remarkable. "Jesus wept" (v. 35).

As he looked upon the tearstained faces of the people before him and listened to their sobs, he felt the depths of their sorrow, and he cried with them.

He simply wept, knowing the outcome but drawing close to the brokenhearted and crushed spirits around him.

"See how he loved him!" the people cried, while others asked the obvious question: "Could not he who opened the eyes of the blind man have kept this man from dying?" (vv. 36–37). The confused crowd was about to learn just what Jesus was capable of.

Notice that Martha and Mary both ran out to meet Jesus, but Mary's posture was different. She fell at his feet. This doesn't mean she was better than Martha, but it could reveal an intimacy and humility that broke open the heart of Jesus. We will see Mary at the feet of Jesus again, literally, in the very next chapter.

But we cannot miss this: the place to go when we are confused and discouraged, when we are mad at God or filled with sadness, is the feet of Jesus.

Right on Time

As Jesus made his way to the tomb, weeping, he asked Mary and Martha to take away the stone that sealed the grave. I imagine for the sisters this was like pouring alcohol into an open wound. He was four days too late. He was also breaking Jewish protocol by getting near a dead body, making himself unclean.

Plus, more than the pain of seeing their brother's dead body, there were logistics to consider.

"But, Lord," Martha interjected, "by this time there is a bad odor, for he has been there four days" (v. 39). Lazarus was very dead. So dead that his body had begun to rot, and the smell was no longer masked by the oils and spices used when they wrapped the body.

This is Martha's way of trying to talk Jesus out of going in to the tomb. But Jesus wasn't going in. Lazarus was coming out.

"Did I not tell you that if you *believe*, you will see the glory of God?" he asked (v. 40). Reluctantly obeying his words, they rolled away the heavy stone enclosing Lazarus's corpse in the tomb.

Then Jesus began to pray to his Father, turning his head and his heart heavenward. "Father," he cried out, "I thank you that you have heard me. I knew that you always hear me, but I said this for the benefit of the people standing here, *that they may believe* that you sent me" (vv. 41–42).

What he was about to do, he was doing *so that they would believe in him.* Then Jesus said the words that would change everything: "Lazarus, come out!" (v. 43).

The people were astounded, because the second Jesus uttered his command for the dead man to rise, it happened.

A dead man drew in a resurrected breath.

Lazarus, who had been dead for the better half of a week, laid to rest and wrapped in burial cloth in a sealed tomb, was alive again. Moving. Breathing. It was impossible, yet there he stood.

As he stumbled out of the tomb, Lazarus looked like a mummy from a haunted house, but there were no theatrics involved. In John's words, "the dead man came out, his hands and feet wrapped with strips of linen, and a cloth around his face" (v. 44). Remember, John, who tells this story, was himself an eyewitness to all of this.

Then Jesus instructed them, "Take off the grave clothes and let him go" (v. 44).

Jesus wants us to do more than exist. He wants us to truly live. He wants us to experience freedom, not bondage. He wants to remove the restrictions, the grave clothes, from our lives.

It wasn't enough for Lazarus to simply be alive. What good was a resurrection if he was still tied up like a mummy? Jesus

> *Jesus wants us to do more than exist. He wants us to truly live. He wants us to experience freedom, not bondage.*

wants the same thing for you, to cut you loose from the regrets of your past and the shame of your mistakes. He wants an abundant life for you filled with joy and purpose and hope.

When you are reborn, old things are cut away from your life.

Standing at the Empty Tomb

Did you notice Jesus specified "Lazarus" in his command to come out? Because Jesus had authority over death, if he'd simply issued a generic command of "Come out!" every dead body on planet Earth would have reanimated and appeared!

The people knew Jesus was a miracle worker, but this was another level. This wasn't resuscitation. It was resurrection.

Skeptics of Jesus became full-fledged followers while others were frightened by his power and fled to Jerusalem to tell the chief priests and Pharisees what they'd encountered. No one, though, could deny what they'd witnessed with their own eyes.

Now the two-day delay suddenly made sense. Jesus had a purpose in his plan.

Whatever circumstances you walk through, no matter how hopeless the situation might seem or how dark the night gets, you're in his capable hands.

Not only does Jesus hold your future but he also knows your heart. Jesus wept openly with his friends. He didn't rebuke them for their disappointment or scold them for mourning. He leaned in close and cried with them. If there's ever a moment where you question if he understands your pain or even cares, the shortest verse in Scripture sums it up succinctly. John 11:35: "Jesus wept."

Jesus gets it. He knows your pain, he mourns your loss, and he weeps with you. Why? Because you're the one he loves, like Lazarus.

Still Raising the Dead . . . at 13,000 Feet

The word *resurrection* took on a new meaning for me in 1998.

I recruited a handful of friends to accompany me on a mission trip to the Himalayas. We would attempt to backpack into a few small villages of Tibetan Buddhists in northern India. As far as we knew, if we were able to reach the Zanskar valley by traveling along the Kashmiri border with Pakistan, we would be the first missionaries to ever reach that area. Our plan was to pack in small, mobile medical clinics. While there we would distribute Bibles and gospel picture books in the local language. We were warned, however, that there was severe fighting along the border and we would have to drive through Kashmir, and there was a chance we could be bombed, taken hostage, or killed.

We spent all summer preparing by hiking with heavy backpacks and taking ice-cold showers. We read books on Tibetan Buddhism and prayed and fasted for God to make a way for us to get to the Zanskar valley, and particularly to a small village called Zangla.

When we arrived, we acclimatized for three days, then loaded our gear (medical supplies, tents, backpacks, Bibles, and storybooks) into a large vehicle that would carry us all the way through the town of Khargill, which sat on the Indian side of the border with Pakistan. The locals said if we were going to be killed, it would be in Khargill.

Every day we prayed for God to make a way for us to get to the Zanskar valley. We asked for miracles. We kept praying specifically that we could take the gospel along with our medical clinic to the village of Zangla.

We approached Khargill several days later and saw a plume of black smoke rising from the town. Directly across the river was a ridge of high mountains: the disputed territory between India and Pakistan, controlled by Islamic militants.

An Indian soldier with a big gun stopped us and refused to let us go into Khargill. He told us there had just been a bombing across the river. After some conversation, and a small gift of 40 rupees, the Indian soldier agreed to let our vehicle pass. We drove right past the buildings that had been bombed just moments earlier. People had been killed. We wondered if they would launch more mortars while we were there. But we had a flat tire, and Khargill was the only place to get it fixed before we continued toward Zangla. We had no choice but to stop and wait for the repair.

We rushed out of Khargill once the tire was fixed and, as we were leaving, our driver pulled over to the side of the road to pick up a hitchhiker. I protested, since none of us knew this man. The driver said he knew him and that he was very important. As a matter of fact, he was a king.

I raised my voice, demanding that we make this man get out of our vehicle. Our lives were in danger; we had just seen dead bodies being dragged from a building. There was no way this man was a king. While I was talking, the hitchhiker looked at me and said, in broken English, "You are a very loud talking boy."

So I spoke directly to him and said, "Sir, I am sorry, but if you are really a king, what are you the king of, and why were you standing on the side of the road trying to hitch a ride?"

What Are the Odds?

He said, "My name is Raja Norbu and I am the king of the *Zanskar valley.* I live in a small village called *Zangla.* It is far from here and difficult to reach. As a provincial official, I must attend annual meetings in Delhi. I was on my way there when my vehicle broke down. Your driver recognized me as King Norbu. That is why he is giving me a lift."

We looked at each other, dumbfounded. He claimed to be the king of the very place we were trying to go and our driver knew it was him, which is why he'd invited him in. This man could give us permission to take the gospel to his village.

Then he asked me my name. "My name is Clayton King," I said. His eyes lit up, and he clasped his hands together and said, "Oh, my friend, yes, you are also a king in your country!" Because my last name was King, and because in his culture a person's last name is indicative of their vocation or identity, he assumed I was a king, literally.

When he asked me what we were doing there in Khargill, I told him the truth, that we were trying to reach his village to hold free medical clinics and give people our holy book, the Bible.

He evidently liked the idea, and in a show of respect and hospitality, he took out a pen and asked for a piece of paper. He wrote a personal letter and handed it to me. I asked him what it said, because I couldn't read Ladakhi. He said, "I want you and your people to go to Zangla without any trouble. This letter will ensure you safe passage there if anyone tries to stop you. Give this letter to my wife. She will take care of you. I have written that you are going to be the king of Zanskar until I return from Delhi next month."

Umm . . . what?

To honor me as a visiting king from America, he made me the temporary king of his region, gave us guaranteed safe passage to his village, and instructed his wife to give us whatever we needed for our medical clinic.

> "Give this letter to my wife. She will take care of you. I have written that you are going to be the king of Zanskar until I return from Delhi next month."

Several days later we arrived in Zangla. It was a village of less than one hundred people. The Himalayas towered on both sides of the valley, and the village clung to the edge of a cliff. I found the queen by showing the letter to the first man I met. He took me to her modest home. Then they made me butter tea and bowed and welcomed me as the interim king of Zangla.

Our team set up camp and prepped for the clinic. There was a steady stream of people all day as we treated everything from boils to cysts to pneumonia. We made fast friends with everyone who came, handed out Bibles and gospel picture books, and then, as the sun sank behind the snow-capped peaks, we began to pack up our medical gear for the day. Then I noticed the queen walking toward our tents. She had a strange look on her face.

She said, "Did you have a good day today helping my people? Did you have everything you needed?" I assured her that we were so happy to be there and appreciated her kindness and hospitality, and when I paused, she said, "Raja, do you know how to deliver a baby?"

Again. Umm . . . what?

A Crazy Prayer and a Stillborn Baby

Of course, I had no idea how to deliver a baby. From what I'd seen on *Little House on the Prairie*, I knew you needed to boil water and get towels. And that was all I knew. However—fortunately—we had a medical doctor on our team who had delivered plenty of babies. The queen said to come quickly because a woman in their village had been in labor for more than a day and she was afraid she would die soon.

With headlamps and emergency supplies, we followed the queen to a small hut where dozens of people were gathered. They were burning incense and chanting. In the corner was a tiny Ladakhi woman lying on sacks and blankets, with blood and water on the floor. The villagers were taking their Tibetan scriptures and touching them to her head while chanting prayers for her and her baby to be okay.

Our doctor examined the mother and informed us she was pregnant with twins and the first baby was breech. That was why the mother couldn't give birth. If she couldn't turn the baby soon and get both babies out, the mother would die. She also said she thought the first baby was already dead in the womb. Then she asked us all to pray. The villagers were superstitious, and if the mother or the babies died, they may think that we'd brought bad luck upon them and perhaps want to do us harm or kill us.

Of course, I had no idea how to deliver a baby. From what I'd seen on Little House on the Prairie, *I knew you needed to boil water and get towels. And that was all I knew.*

Did God really bring us to Zangla to fail? Did God really allow me to be named the interim king of the Zanskar valley as a way for us to get there and share the gospel, only to have this mother die in childbirth and the villagers blame us?

By this time the entire village had arrived to see if we could do this. We'd told them all about our God that day at the clinic. We'd given them Bibles and spoke of the power of Jesus. Could it be that God had allowed us to now show them his power immediately after telling them who he was? I assumed that this was exactly what God was doing, so I prayed out loud and asked our driver to interpret it for everyone who had gathered in the room and at the door and the windows.

"Tell them that our God is Jesus Christ, who was killed for our sins and then rose from the dead. He is powerful and loving, and he will show you his power. This mother will live tonight. And these babies will live tonight. God sent us to you for this purpose. If they die, then you can do whatever you wish to us."

I heard myself saying the words but couldn't remember actually planning to say any of them. Then I wondered what would happen if the baby was already dead in the womb. *Too late now.* God would do whatever God wanted to do, and we would be there to see the results.

The doctor asked me to stay by her side during the delivery. We had to break the baby's leg at the hip to get him to turn. Finally, after four hours he was born, but he was born dead. It was a stillbirth.

We all held our breath. There was no telling how long he had been dead. No breath, no pulse, no heartbeat. Nothing. And we were on the hook for it. We panicked and prayed for

God to get us out of there alive, to do something to fix the situation. All the villagers watched us.

And while we were praying, I heard a baby scream.

I looked down and the little baby boy—who was born dead—was screaming at the top of his lungs as our doctor held him. He was alive! God raised that baby from the dead, and the entire village saw it happen, while we prayed.

I looked down and the little baby boy—who was born dead—was screaming at the top of his lungs as our doctor held him. He was alive!

We wrapped him in my T-shirt, then the doctor splinted his broken hip with duct tape and popsicle sticks. An hour later his twin brother was born. He was fine and healthy. We gave the mother an IV drip and she fell asleep on the floor while the women of the village tended to the twins. We then packed up our gear and received many thanks from the villagers who had witnessed the miracle.

We walked back to our camp around midnight, but I didn't go to sleep. I laid outside my tent looking at the stars, my body filled with adrenaline and my heart about to burst with the thought of what we had just seen God do among these people.

He had raised the dead. And he did it so they would believe.

So That We All Might Believe

The people of Zangla are Tibetan Buddhists. They don't believe in God, but they fear evil spirits and demons. Often in cultures like theirs, the most effective way for the gospel to be understood is called "a show of power." This is where the traditional form of belief comes face-to-face with the proclamation of the gospel that Jesus is Lord. Spiritualist cultures respond to the power, or the god, who can prove itself most powerful in a showdown.

I believe that's exactly what happened in Zangla. The people had never heard of Jesus. We arrived and told them that our God would show himself to them. Within a few hours, God provided an opportunity for them to actually see what we had just proclaimed.

It would have been just as easy for God to let the first baby be delivered healthy, but it wouldn't have made the same impression as the baby being born dead and then seeing God bring the baby back to life. It's similar to the people in Bethany who knew Jesus could heal the sick but needed to see him raise the dead.

A Monk, Reborn

We completed our original mission, which was to leave Bibles for the villagers. One year later, I returned to Zangla with my wife. We'd been married for four months when we began a two-hundred-mile trek to six unreached villages, beginning at Zangla. As we wrapped up our one-day medical clinic there, we saw our driver under the medical tent praying with a Tibetan Buddhist monk. When they finished, he walked him over to us and informed us that the monk wanted to become a follower of Jesus.

This monk had been reading the Bible in his language every day for a year, since we left, and decided that he wanted to follow a God who was strong enough to raise the dead. He had been in the room the night the twins were born. He saw the miracle, and he believed. He wanted to be reborn.

Jesus has great plans for you, and there is nothing in your life that he cannot resurrect. He can use you in miraculous ways, even when you doubt his plan or his timing. There will be lots of waiting. There will also be some weeping. But Jesus gets the final word, even over death.

TEN

The Benefit of Doubt

I don't play golf.

I have better things to do, like take a nap, clip my toenails, or watch reruns of *Andy Griffith* online. I'd honestly rather sit and do nothing than play golf. I like to watch golf. It's better than Ambien and puts me to sleep in two minutes flat.

Suffice it to say I have no context for the sport or the superstars who play it. Oh, sure, I know who Tiger Woods is, and I've heard of Jack Nicklaus. Oh, yeah—and Happy Gilmore. There you have it: the extent of my golf knowledge.

So it makes sense now, looking back on it, that I had no idea who was sitting across the table from me that night.

Our church had just hosted a one-day leadership conference, and some pretty well-known pastors had spoken, like Andy Stanley, Francis Chan, Mark Driscoll, Craig Groeschel, and Judah Smith. In the church world, they would classify as famous. When the day ended, a group of us gathered for dinner at Sullivans, a terrific restaurant in Anderson, and the table was full of some of these pastors.

Sharie and I knew everyone at the table except for one couple. Because of the world I live in, I'm aware of all the influential church leaders and, as a general rule, I know what they look like. This couple wasn't registering at all. I was too embarrassed to ask their names. So we just sat there, listening, observing, and wondering who they were.

I'd honestly rather sit and do nothing than play golf. I like to watch golf. It's better than Ambien and puts me to sleep in two minutes flat.

The husband talked a lot about watching *The Dukes of Hazzard*. He was from the panhandle of Florida. And he liked to play golf. He and I talked about pro wrestling too. He grew up watching the same guys I used to watch like Ric Flair, Ricky Steamboat, and Dusty Rhodes. I decided that I really liked this guy. He had an awesome Southern accent. And his wife was tall, played basketball, and was very sweet too.

Several months later I came home from preaching somewhere on a Sunday afternoon. Exhausted from a day spent in airports and crazy traffic, I kissed my wife and kids, plopped down in the recliner, and turned on the TV. I clicked through a few channels and found what I was looking for: golf. I knew I'd break a world record for how fast a human can fall asleep. But before I started snoring, the screen filled with a shot of a man's face. He was wearing a hat and was about to swing a club at the golf ball. And based on the commentary of Jim Nance, this was a pretty important shot.

Then it hit me. I knew that guy! I called Sharie into the den and said, "Isn't that the guy we ate dinner with at Sullivans? His wife was taller than him and played basketball, and he liked Ric Flair." She responded, "Wow, yeah, that is him! So, I guess he's a golfer if he's playing golf on TV, huh?"

While we were talking, that man hit the ball, and it was some kind of crazy shot, and the announcers went crazy, and a moment later he won the golf tournament.

He won The Masters. In Augusta, Georgia. The Super Bowl of golf. The biggest golf tournament on earth. His name was Bubba Watson. We watched him win his first Masters that afternoon. He won another Masters two years later in 2014. We'd spent two hours at a table with him and his lovely wife, Angie, and had no idea he was famous because we had no idea who he was.

That's my Bubba Watson story, but for many of us that's our Jesus story. He surprises us in crazy ways we don't see coming. We don't always recognize him or see what he's up to. We have tons of questions and a boatload of doubts when things go sideways in our lives. But he's always right there with us, even if it takes us a while to recognize who he is and what he's doing.

When it dawned on us that we'd spent significant time with a really amazing man without knowing who he was, the first thought that occurred to me was how similar this was to a story in Luke 24, which happens to be my favorite story about Jesus.

Jesus had been brutally crucified. His followers were terrified. They watched as he was arrested on Thursday night, executed, and buried in a borrowed tomb before sundown on Friday. Saturday was filled with silence.

Then came Sunday and rumors of the impossible: resurrection.

But many doubted.

The benefit that doubt brings in your life is that when you're at your lowest, it sets up the surprise moment where Jesus reveals himself, his plan, his provision, and how he was playing the long game the whole time. We all doubt because we're all human. Doubt is a natural emotion that invites the supernatural power and presence of Jesus.

Resurrection Sunday

With the assistance of Nicodemus, one of Jesus's followers named Joseph of Arimathea prepared Jesus for burial and placed him in his own tomb. On that Sunday morning, a group of Jesus's female followers made their way to where they thought his body would be.

The Galilean women had followed Joseph there, and after seeing where Jesus was buried, they'd prepared perfumes and spices for him. Because Jewish law required the people to rest on the Sabbath, they couldn't anoint his body on Saturday. They had to wait until Sunday morning to venture to the tomb.

They expected to find the same scene as the one they'd encountered two days before: a heavy stone sealing the entrance and armed Roman soldiers standing guard. What they did discover changed everything. The stone, which would take several strong men to move, had been rolled away from the entryway. The women simply walked inside.

Instead of finding a lifeless corpse, they saw only remnants of the burial clothes he'd been wrapped in—and a pair of angels, who gleamed like lightning. As I heard Andy Stanley say once, nobody expected no body. To say the women were afraid is an understatement, as they bowed in reverence before them. The angels, though, had good news, along with a reminder of a few promises Jesus had made while he was among them.

"Why do you look for the living among the dead?" the angels asked, then proclaimed jubilantly, "He is not here; he has risen!" (Luke 24:5–6).

What? They'd been at Golgotha just two days ago. They'd watched him die. They'd heard him cry out from the cross, "Father, into your hands I commit my spirit" (23:46), and watched with their own eyes as Jesus closed his for the last time.

The next word the angels uttered was enough to silence all of the women's doubts and confusion: *remember*. "Remember how he told you, while he was still with you in Galilee, 'The Son of Man must be delivered over to the hands of sinners, be crucified and on the third day be raised again'" (24:7).

Luke tells us that immediately "they remembered his words" (v. 8).

The women bolted back to town to find the disciples and the rest of Jesus's followers, eager to share the mind-blowing news of his resurrection. He was alive! But the disciples didn't put much stock in the women's testimony. They doubted their story.

"They did not believe the women, because their words seemed to them like nonsense" (v. 11). These men were upside-down emotionally. Their rabbi had been murdered. They assumed they were next. So they were hiding out, hoping the authorities didn't come for them.

But, like the women, the disciples just needed to remember. Jesus had told them this would happen.

In the midst of their doubt, Peter got up and ran to the tomb to see if what the women said was true. Sprinting to the grave, Peter found the same scene the women had described (minus the angels). The stone was rolled away from the door, the strips of Jesus's burial clothes were lying neatly on the ground, and there was no dead body. While he wasn't quite sure what had happened to Jesus, one thing was certain: the tomb really was empty.

It brings Jesus great joy to do something so good for you that it leaves you speechless.

Do you see how many surprises there are in this story? Like a parent loves to surprise their kids, or like a husband or wife surprises their spouse with an anniversary or birthday gift, it brings Jesus great joy to do something so good for you that it leaves you speechless.

The Long Walk Back to Emmaus

That was Sunday morning, the first Easter. Not long after Peter stood dumbfounded at the empty tomb, a follower of Christ named Cleopas left Jerusalem with his friend to walk home to Emmaus. They would have plenty of time to discuss all that was on their minds, considering the seven-mile trek to Emmaus would take hours on foot.

These men were mourning. And they were doubting. They had a lot to talk about.

They had likely ventured to Jerusalem expecting another typical Passover celebration, intermingled with teachings and maybe a few miracles from Jesus. Instead, they saw him dragged away, whipped and beaten, and murdered even though he had committed no crime.

Then Mary and Joanna and a few other women had burst in that morning spouting off about angels at the tomb and a resurrection. That had to be wishful thinking, a comforting delusion in the face of the heartbreaking reality that Jesus was dead.

But then there were Peter and John to consider. They'd said the tomb was empty as well. It seemed irrational, almost absurd. But *what if?*

As Cleopas and his friend walked home to Emmaus, probably also walking through all the possible explanations for what had happened in Jerusalem, they were joined by another traveler, a man they knew but failed to recognize at first.

As they walked and talked, verbalizing their doubts and confusion, "Jesus himself came up and walked along with them" (Luke 24:15).

He saw their hurt and he sought their hearts, taking the time to reach through to them even in their doubt. Their meeting was no coincidence; Scripture tells us that the men were initially "kept from recognizing him" (v. 16).

This wasn't the first time that day Jesus snuck up on someone who loved him without them recognizing him.

When Mary went to the tomb and found it empty, Jesus appeared to her right outside the opening. She thought he was the gardener or the caretaker until he spoke. She recognized his voice and knew it was Jesus when he called her by her name (John 20:15–16).

Now he's walking with two of his other disciples and, like Mary, they have no clue it's Jesus. "What are you discussing together as you walk along?" (Luke 24:17), Jesus asked, knowing full well what they were discussing.

With their heads hanging low and their hearts filled with sorrow, Cleopas asked Jesus, "Are you the only one visiting Jerusalem who does not know the things that have happened there in these days?" (v. 18). In other words, *Do you live under a rock? Where have you been?*

How could anyone who had been even in the vicinity of Jerusalem that weekend possibly question what was on their minds? It was the same thing on everyone's mind—Jesus of Nazareth! Yet much to Cleopas's surprise, the stranger proceeded with his questions, appearing to genuinely be in the dark.

"What things?" Jesus probed, encouraging Cleopas to put the weekend's events into his own words (v. 19). Jesus is setting them up for the big surprise by pretending to be clueless.

"About Jesus of Nazareth," they replied. "He was a prophet, powerful in word and deed before God and all the people" (v. 19).

They were talking about Jesus to Jesus, completely blind to the fact that they were walking right beside him. They were literally preaching the gospel of Jesus Christ to Jesus Christ. They'd witnessed his miracles, sat under his teachings, and been saturated with his Word—they never should have questioned his resurrection for a second.

Yet there they were, trudging back to their daily routine instead of simply believing the words Christ himself had spoken just days earlier.

Jesus could have rebuked them for doubting his promise, but instead he walked with them and talked with them. On the most prolific day in human history, the resurrected Son of God was orchestrating the details behind the scenes to meet a couple of ordinary men in the middle of their doubts and confusion.

If you wanted to start a religion and have people follow you, wouldn't you appear on the steps of the temple in Jerusalem three days after the entire city watched you die? That's how you build momentum! You show up alive after your enemies killed you and watch people by the millions chant your name and pledge their lives to you.

But not Jesus. He did the exact opposite of what he should do to capitalize off the momentum of the moment. Instead of staging a massive pep rally in the city, he left the city behind to hang out with two guys heading home to their families, filled with questions and grief.

They said, "The chief priests and our rulers handed him over to be sentenced to death, and they crucified him; but we had hoped that he was the one who was going to redeem Israel" (vv. 20–21).

"But we had hoped." They truly believed Jesus would be the one to save the people, the one prophesied for centuries. How could he redeem Israel if he was dead?

But Jesus was up to something! The reason we're often surprised by his plans is that we lack the ability to know all the things he knows and lack the power to do all the things he does to orchestrate his grand schemes. And all his schemes are good, bringing him glory and giving us life and joy. We can look back and see some of his plans, but we can't see them looking forward. We just have to trust him.

As the men walked on, they continued to fill Jesus in on what had occurred since his death a few days earlier, explaining,

> What is more, it is the third day since all this took place. In addition, some of our women amazed us. They went to the tomb early this morning but didn't find his body. They came and told us that they had seen a vision of angels, who said he was alive. Then some of our companions went to the tomb and found it just as the women had said, but they did not see Jesus. (vv. 21–24)

The empty tomb and the pile of burial clothes were definitely odd and perplexing, but not enough to sway them into believing the impossible. What if someone had stolen his body? Because they hadn't seen Jesus or the tomb with their own eyes, they struggled to believe.

A Call to Remember

When we're wrestling with doubt and wondering if Jesus is really paying attention to the details of our lives, the very best thing we can do is *remember*. Think back to the answered prayers. Recall the moments we've felt his presence. Rehearse the times he came through for us or someone we love. And remember the promises of Scripture, the verses and stories we read from the Bible. It's so easy to forget when we're distracted by doubts.

Just like the angels reminded the women at the tomb, Jesus jogged their memory that day:

> And he said to them, "O foolish ones, and slow of heart to believe all that the prophets have spoken! Was it not necessary that the Christ should suffer these things and enter into his glory?" And beginning with Moses and all the Prophets, he interpreted to them in all the Scriptures the things concerning himself. (vv. 25–27 ESV)

Jesus took the time to walk them through every word ever spoken of him in all of Scripture. It's all part of his setup for the surprise.

Jesus reminded them of Micah's promise that he would be born in Bethlehem, of Isaiah's prophecy of the virgin birth, and of Deuteronomy's vision of a prophet who was to come out of the people of Israel.

He mapped out Scripture's prophecies right up to his death and resurrection, from his triumphant welcome to Jerusalem on the back of a donkey in Zechariah 9:9 to the rejection and hatred he received from his own people in Isaiah 53.

The more details from Scripture he laid out, the more it all made sense. Even Judas's betrayal was foretold in Zechariah 11, right down to the price of thirty pieces of silver he put on Jesus's life.

He would have taken them to the prophet Isaiah's words about his crucifixion, telling them how he "took up our pain and bore our suffering," and how "he was pierced for our transgressions, he was crushed for our iniquities; the punishment that brought us peace was on him, and by his wounds we are healed" (Isa. 53:4–5).

He would have reminded them of David's words in the Psalms, of how they would spit at him, mock him, pierce his hands and feet, and cast lots for his clothes as they did at the foot of the cross.

He shared Isaiah's prophecy that he would be buried in a rich man's tomb, just as he had been laid to rest in Joseph of Arimathea's grave.

He also would have reminded them of his own words, handed down to us in Matthew 12, where he prophesied his own death and resurrection: "For as Jonah was three days and three nights in the belly of a huge fish, so the Son of Man will be three days and three nights in the heart of the earth" (v. 40).

The men had no idea when they said, "It is the third day since all this took place" (Luke 24:21) just how significant his timing was—not until they spent some time in the presence of their risen Redeemer.

Rather than being left to drown in their doubt, they got an all-day personal Bible study—from the Person who authored the Bible.

We often assume God gets angry with us when we have questions. Nothing could be further from the truth. He welcomes them. He wants us to ask, and God will answer us based on our ability to understand. He can't tell us everything, but he can tell us something.

If Jesus was willing to chase down these two guys just to explain the reasons for his death and resurrection, don't you think he's happy to hear what you've been questioning in your head and heart?

The Scars Tell the Story

In response to his teaching, the men were enthralled by him. They asked this "stranger" to stay for dinner, and he did. No matter how dense or doubtful you are, when you invite Jesus in, he accepts.

As they sat down to eat, Jesus blessed the food, broke the bread, and handed it to them—and in an instant, "their eyes were opened and they recognized him" (Luke 24:31).

All day long, Jesus was setting up the surprise!

A seven-mile walk would take between four and six hours, depending on age and level of fitness. They walked and talked for miles with Jesus without recognizing him, yet the moment he broke bread in their home, his identity was illuminated.

The symbolism in their realization of Jesus's presence is so incredibly rich. The bread of life, who was broken for them three days earlier, was now sitting at their supper table, resurrected and in the flesh, literally breaking bread for them.

But there was another element involved in their discovery, and it stems in part from another of Jesus's appearances around this time.

John 20 recounts the moment Thomas, one of the twelve disciples, came to believe Jesus truly conquered death.

Thomas couldn't bring himself to believe Jesus was alive, even after the other disciples had seen him for themselves. He told his friends, "Unless I see the nail marks in his hands and put my finger where the nails were, and put my hand into his side, I will not believe" (John 20:25). The nickname stuck— Doubting Thomas.

A week after he made that proclamation, Thomas got the shock of his life as Jesus appeared out of thin air in the middle of the room—with the doors locked and the curtains drawn— proclaiming, "Peace be with you!" (v. 26).

Rather than rebuke Thomas and push him away, Jesus came closer, giving him the exact proof he'd asked for. "Put your finger here," he said. "See my hands. Reach out your hand and put it into my side. Stop doubting and believe" (v. 27).

Eventually, our doubts give way to faith, because faith replaces fear. But not without a fight.

Eventually, our doubts give way to faith, because faith replaces fear. But not without a fight.

I believe the same nail-scarred hands that Thomas touched were on full display when Jesus faced Cleopas and his friend across the table and broke bread with them, removing any shadow of a doubt of who he was.

The pierced hands that Isaiah and David had alluded to so many years ago, the ones that bore the weight of the sins of the world, were serving them. His scars told the story. They bore witness to a crucifixion and a resurrection.

Imagine yourself sitting at this table. Jesus breaks the bread. He reaches toward you. He turns his hands palm-up to hand you the broken pieces. He exposes his wrists for you to see. Undeniable holes in his flesh testify that this was no mere man. No one had ever survived a crucifixion. Everyone nailed to a cross died. No one walked around with those scars.

It was the scars on his wrists from the crucifixion that opened their eyes. And their hearts. He had been with them the whole time!

As soon as the men recognized Jesus, "he disappeared from their sight" (Luke 24:31), leaving them completely in awe.

"Were not our hearts burning within us while he talked with us on the road and opened the Scriptures to us?" they said (v. 32).

With their hearts ablaze after recognizing the risen Jesus, they turned right around and headed back the way they'd just come to tell everyone. They had to walk all the way back to the city in the dark—but they were no longer in the dark.

As soon as they arrived, they explained to the eleven "how Jesus was recognized by them when he broke the bread" (v. 35). But there was one more surprise in store for them.

As they told the story to the disciples, in that same breath Jesus appeared to them all, urging them to look at the scars on his hands and feet. He was serious about showing them his scars. He wanted to prove to them all, finally, that he was alive.

Your scars can be more than a reminder of a painful accident. They can testify to the surprising power of Jesus to heal you. You can show your scars as proof that you've been reborn by the power of the cross. You can point others to the gospel as you point out the places in your life where Jesus has touched you, healed you, and brought life. A scar is more than a place you were hurt. It's a place you were healed.

So Close You Can Touch Him

Rather than revealing himself on a grand stage to the masses in the city, Jesus spent Resurrection Sunday with two lowly guys on their daily commute, meeting their doubt with proof.

They were side by side with Jesus, literally close enough to reach out and touch him. What does this say about Jesus? It shows that he sees and pursues everyone, not just the powerful, the rich, the religious, or the influential.

How many times have we missed Jesus because we couldn't look past a problem we were facing?

Maybe you've been around Jesus your entire life. You know what Scripture says about him. But here's the truth: you can be the most knowledgeable person in the room but unless you've encountered him for yourself, all that knowledge is worthless.

If you invite him into your heart like these men invited him into their home, even in your doubt and confusion, he will come in. He always comes where he's invited.

The men on the road to Emmaus were not there by accident. They thought they were walking away from Christ, but he was with them all along, pursuing them with a love so fierce that it conquered death to get to them.

That same intentional love is pursuing you today. Open your eyes, see the nail-scarred hands reaching out to you, and invite him in.

ELEVEN

How Resistance Reveals Jesus

Being reborn guarantees you some things: eternal life, abundant life, a peace that passes understanding, assurance of salvation, the unconditional love of God, and a place in God's family forever.

Being reborn does not guarantee good grades, a job promotion, perfect health, a full scholarship, the perfect marriage, perfect kids, early retirement, a stress-free life, the applause of others, or popularity.

The apostle Paul put it bluntly: "In fact, everyone who wants to live a godly life in Christ Jesus will be persecuted" (2 Tim. 3:12).

Jesus summed it up in Matthew 5:11–12: "You are blessed when they insult you and persecute you and falsely say every kind of evil against you because of me. Be glad and rejoice, because your reward is great in heaven. For that is how they persecuted the prophets who were before you" (CSB).

With this in mind, it must've been unreal to be a follower of Christ in the first days following his resurrection. Each believer had a unique conversion story, putting their faith in Jesus at different times during his ministry and after his ascension.

His followers watched as he ascended into heaven, leaving them with a promise and a commission: they would "receive power when the Holy Spirit comes on you," and would "be my witnesses in Jerusalem, and in all Judea and Samaria, and to the ends of the earth" (Acts 1:8).

Can you imagine being alive and bearing witness to the most important events in all of human history? Then to see his promise fulfilled as the Holy Spirit fell upon the believers at Pentecost, proving that God and his power still remained with them, even though Jesus had returned to his rightful place in heaven (Acts 2)?

Filled with the Holy Spirit, his followers began to preach the gospel zealously and perform miracles in his name. Word of Jesus's resurrection spread like wildfire.

But there was another way the gospel spread: persecution.

None of us want to be persecuted for our faith. We'd rather avoid pain and suffering if possible. Yet there is a sense in which the glory of God is revealed in a special way, and people are strangely drawn to the kingdom of God, when they see Christians endure hardship with grace and patience. As the church founders said in the early centuries of the church, the blood of the martyrs is the seed of the church. The world that often attempts to silence the gospel is the same world that watches our actions when we suffer.

An Unstoppable Force

The church expanded with thousands of people devoting their lives to Jesus. It was a moving scene, as Peter, John, and the other disciples continued in Jesus's footsteps, healing multitudes of people and proclaiming the good news.

But not everyone was thrilled with the flourishing church. The rage of the religious establishment intensified when his body disappeared after his crucifixion and hundreds of people claimed to have seen him resurrected.

Now his ragtag team of disciples was back at it again, but with boldness. They'd bounced back after Jesus's death, undaunted. They'd even replaced Judas, who'd betrayed Jesus.

Carrying out the Great Commission in the wake of Jesus's departure was dangerous. Like all of Jesus's promises, the declaration that his followers would suffer for his sake and face persecution in his name would also come true. Yet instead of squashing the Christian movement, the Sanhedrin's actions only seemed to fuel it.

While the disciples preached and healed and ministered to the poor, the members of the Sanhedrin arrested them, flogged them, and forbid them from speaking in Jesus's name. But no matter how many people were threatened or beaten or executed, they couldn't be stopped.

The church grew then, and grows now, when it's persecuted. Hard times make us holy. We grow when we're stretched and challenged. We're forced to really rely on Jesus when our faith is tested.

Full of Grace and Power

As the church grew, the twelve disciples found themselves wearing too many hats, so they elected seven men to take over managing the distribution of food to the poor. One of those men, Stephen, refused to back down, risking everything for

Jesus. We don't know many details about Stephen's backstory, but Acts 6:5 tells us all we need to know, stating that he was "a man full of faith and of the Holy Spirit."

We also know that Stephanos, a Greek name meaning *witness*, had his heart set on sharing the gospel with the Greek people as well as Hebrews. Stephen saw people the way Jesus did, and he proclaimed the gospel to the gentiles, not just the Jews.

Scripture tells us that Stephen, "full of God's grace and power, performed great wonders and signs among the people," and in response, he angered "members of the Synagogue of the Freedman . . . Jews of Cyrene and Alexandria as well as the province of Cilicia and Asia" (vv. 8–9). That's a lot of ticked off people.

But despite their best efforts, "they could not stand up against the wisdom the Spirit gave him as he spoke" (v. 10).

So, just like they'd done with Jesus, they schemed and fabricated allegations against Stephen, concocting a plan to gather a group of false witnesses. It was all they could do to halt the impact of Stephen's words (vv. 11–14).

These men claimed that they had heard Stephen speaking blasphemy against Moses and God, and the religious wingnuts snapped to action. They dragged him before their version of the Jedi Council, arguing with Stephen over his theology and accusing him like they'd accused Jesus months earlier.

Notice how the followers of Jesus in the Bible are often treated like Jesus was treated. Can the same be said for us? Do we ever feel the sting of rejection or the blunt force of being mocked for our faith?

Not once in the Bible did a Christian ever complain about losing their rights when they were persecuted for their faith. Instead, they saw it as an opportunity to be more bold with the message of the gospel. Is that how we react when we feel we're being persecuted?

Faith on Trial

As Stephen faced the Sanhedrin, the lies began. "This fellow never stops speaking against this holy place and against the law," they claimed (v. 13). "For we have heard him say that this Jesus of Nazareth will destroy this place and change the customs Moses handed down to us" (v. 14).

The chief priest asked Stephen if the charges were true. Now it was his turn to testify.

He could've renounced Jesus and escaped with a less severe punishment if he'd approached the council with reverence and stroked their egos. But with his life on the

> Not once in the Bible did a Christian ever complain about losing their rights when they were persecuted for their faith. Instead, they saw it as an opportunity to be more bold with the message of the gospel.

line, Stephen began to proclaim the story of the gospel and "they saw that his face was like the face of an angel" (v. 15).

"Brothers and fathers," he urged them. "Listen to me!" (7:2). Then he proceeded to walk the men in the courtroom through the history of Judaism. Starting with Abraham, he described the births of Isaac and Jacob and the nation of Israel, the plights and redemption of Joseph and his siblings that led the Jewish people into Egypt, and the ventures of Moses and Aaron that led them out. He moved on to Jacob, Joshua, and Solomon, quoting Scripture the entire time.

He spoke of God's faithfulness to their forebears. He reminded the Sanhedrin of the awesome and mighty works God had done. He spoke of God's steadfast forgiveness and providence and the Israelites' lack of faithfulness.

Winding his way to the present, he called out those same actions in the priests before him: "You stiff-necked people!" he cried out. "Your hearts and ears are still uncircumcised" (v. 51). He suggested that they were spiritually blind to their own hypocrisy.

Bringing his message full circle, he passionately proclaimed, "You are just like your ancestors: You always resist the Holy Spirit!" (v. 51). Ouch. Stephen, a Greek, was deconstructing the foundations of their religiosity, calling them out for their pretentious misunderstanding of the Word of God.

He didn't preach the narrative of the Old Testament to shame the Sanhedrin. Instead, it served as his defense. Stephen wasn't blaspheming God and misinterpreting Scripture. His accusers were. He wanted them all to believe in Jesus and be reborn.

Stephen was unrelenting. "Was there ever a prophet your ancestors did not persecute? They even killed those who predicted the coming of the Righteous One. And now you have betrayed and murdered him—you who have received the law that was given through angels but have not obeyed it" (vv. 52–53).

He knew the weight of his words and how hard-hearted and ruthless his audience was. His sermon wouldn't yield a few eye rolls and insults. It would bring death, but he spoke the words anyway. He had been given a gift, and rather than back down, he chose to preach.

Things moved quickly from that point forward. Unable to contain their seething rage, the members of the Sanhedrin "were furious and gnashed their teeth at him" (v. 54). It became clear that Stephen would not be walking out of the court. He would be dragged.

Then, something remarkable happened. While the red-faced, scowling Pharisees were glaring at Stephen, his eyes were focused upward.

While they were watching him, Stephen was watching Jesus. As he looked at the resurrected King, any pain or torture these men could inflict upon him was rendered insignificant.

"Look," he said, mesmerized by the presence of Jesus, "I see heaven open and the Son of Man standing at the right hand of God" (v. 56).

His proclamation sent the members of the Sanhedrin over the edge. "They covered their ears and, yelling at the top of their voices, they all rushed at him, dragged him out of the city and began to stone him" (vv. 57–58).

Even then, as the people violently hurled rocks at him, Stephen prayed, asking Jesus to receive his spirit. Then, falling to his knees, in the last moment of his life, he asked God to forgive his murderers before the final blow ended his life.

Stephen's murder set off a chain reaction, kicking off wide-scale persecution of all the believers in Jerusalem. While many more would follow in his footsteps, Stephen was the first Christian martyr recorded in history, the first person to be murdered for proclaiming the gospel.

Have you ever considered that God can bring a good result from a bad event? What if God could leverage the things that hurt you the most in order to help others find Jesus?

We grow deeply when we suffer greatly, because we see Jesus more clearly in the hardest moments of life.

A Strange Church Growth Strategy

The persecution of the church that followed Stephen's death forced most of the believers in Jerusalem to disperse into the surrounding regions of Judea and Samaria. They carried the message of Jesus along the roads and highways and into every major city in the Roman Empire. This is how the gospel spread and the message of the kingdom advanced worldwide.

We grow deeply when we suffer greatly, because we see Jesus more clearly in the hardest moments of life.

The words of the patriarch Joseph in Genesis 50:20 come to mind: "You intended to harm me, but God intended it for good to accomplish what is now being done, the saving of many lives."

Stephen chose to give his life for something far bigger than himself, something God meant for good. Stephen sacrificed his life in the ultimate act of faithfulness, mirroring Christ every step of the way. He was able to ask forgiveness for his murderers because Jesus had done the exact same thing for his killers just months earlier.

Physically, Jesus had ascended into heaven, his days of walking the earth behind him. There are only a few recorded instances of people encountering Jesus after his ascension, the first of which occurred at Stephen's trial.

Not long before that day, Jesus was murdered by the same people who would drag Stephen away to his death. Jesus knew what Stephen was feeling because Jesus had just experienced it. Rather than leaving Stephen by himself, he chose to split the heavens wide open and smile down at him, to let him know that he was there and he was watching.

Can you imagine? You're standing trial with an unjust judge and jury who want nothing more than to kill you. It's personal for them. As you realize there's no escape and death is just around the corner, you look up to see heaven itself opened before you, and Jesus looking upon you lovingly, signaling that it's all going to be okay.

Looking into the blinding brilliance, Stephen got a glimpse of the glory to come. As he looked upon his loving Father, and into the knowing eyes of his Savior, nothing else mattered. In condemning Stephen to death, the Sanhedrin gave him a preview of the beautiful, eternal future before him.

Just Like Jesus

There's a strong possibility that Stephen had met Jesus face-to-face before he was crucified, or that he'd heard him teach in the temple courts, but we don't know that for sure. We know that he encountered Jesus from a distance at the moment of his murder, and as soon as he died, Jesus was the first to welcome him into heaven.

When the New Testament speaks of Jesus being positioned beside God the Father in heaven, he is always *seated* beside his throne.

Jesus himself said, "You will see the Son of Man *seated* at the right hand of Power and coming with the clouds of heaven" (Mark 14:62 CSB).

Paul says in Colossians 3:1, "So if you have been raised with Christ, seek the things above, where Christ is, *seated* at the right hand of God" (CSB). Ephesians 1:20 and Hebrews 8:1 also describe him as seated at the right hand of the Father.

This was the place of honor and authority, but his posture is the same: sitting down. This doesn't mean he's tired or catching his breath. It means he's in control.

The only time Jesus is ever depicted as *standing* in heaven is the moment just before Stephen dies.

Jesus jumped to his feet to welcome Stephen into his kingdom. The first martyr for the gospel got a standing ovation from the King of Kings.

He was filled with the Holy Spirit like Jesus.

He proclaimed the kingdom of God like Jesus.

He was hated by the religious establishment like Jesus.

He was falsely accused like Jesus.

He prayed for his murderers like Jesus.

He committed his spirit to God at his death like Jesus.

He died like Jesus.

And he was personally welcomed into eternity by Jesus.

Being reborn means that we become more and more like Jesus. The end result of living for Jesus is dying for Jesus. We don't have to die as a martyr, but when we die, we make sure our gaze is fixed toward Jesus. The best way to ensure that is to keep our eyes on Jesus while we live.

From Persecutor to Preacher

I met a man once who changed my life because Jesus had changed his. I think he's a modern-day Stephen.

Ram was named after a deity in his family's religious tradition. His parents were devout, and he pursued their practices and rituals in their village in India. As an adult, he became a police officer, a coveted job that very few achieved.

As he rose through the ranks, he became known as one who fiercely opposed Christianity, to the point of physically persecuting pastors and those who preached the gospel. He arrived one day on the scene where he heard that an evangelist was proclaiming salvation from sin, determined to shut him down, but he was urged by those in the audience to listen to the tall preacher from South India. He did, and his heart was strangely stirred by his words. He decided to approach the man after his message, and when he did, he asked him how he could attain the kind of peace with God that this man had been talking about. And the evangelist, named Thomas, told him how he could be reborn.

Then and there, Ram prayed and confessed his faith in Christ. He opened his heart to the gospel as he encountered the good news that he could begin a brand-new life as a follower of Jesus. Two months later he asked Thomas, the man who led him to faith, to baptize him as he publicly identified himself as a believer. He also changed his name from Ram to Paul on the day of his baptism. He didn't want to be associated with a false god from another religion anymore. He wanted to take the name of the great church planter who encountered Jesus on the road to Damascus and was reborn from a life of persecuting Christians himself.

Little did he know just how much he would have in common with the apostle Paul.

Would You Believe?

Paul sensed God calling him to resign his position with the police to pursue ministry, so he moved his family with him to a Bible college in the north, even though his wife wasn't a Christian. But Jesus had so radically changed her husband that one week before he graduated from Bible college, she asked Jesus to become her Lord. She testified that once Paul became a Christian, he stopped coming home drunk after work and became more loving and kind toward her and their children.

After graduation, Paul and his family traveled back to the city they'd come from to proclaim the gospel, but they were not welcomed. A mob of people who were angry that he'd left his religion to become a Christian did the unthinkable to Paul. They made him eat the dung and drink the urine from a cow. Then they forced battery acid in his mouth and attempted to disembowel him with a sharp stick. He miraculously survived the beating and was nursed back to health.

His family then decided to plant a church in one of the largest cities in India, specifically to reach people from his home state who'd settled there as day laborers. With full knowledge that their lives were in jeopardy, they started a small church and began teaching the Bible.

Some saw this as a threat to their culture, so they demanded that Paul and his family leave. But they remained steadfast and continued to love the people of their city. So one very angry man took matters into his own hands. He instigated a crowd of people to attack Paul's family. This time, however, it wasn't Paul who received the blows. It was his wife and his daughter.

He was forced to watch an angry mob of men brutalize his little girl, then he watched them light both his daughter and his wife on fire. Both died in front of him, burned alive because of their faith in Christ, refusing to deny Jesus or recant their faith.

Traumatized from the unspeakable horror he'd witnessed, Paul spent eight months recovering at the Bible college he'd attended. Little by little, he grew stronger and began to recover. Despite what he had suffered, he wanted to return to the city where his wife and daughter were martyred for their faith. He prayed that he could one day preach the gospel there and offer hope and forgiveness to those who had taken their lives.

Three years later, Paul saw his prayers answered in that very city.

Would you believe that the man who had instigated the mob to attack Paul's family, who had watched as they burned his wife and daughter, came to Paul and asked his forgiveness?

Would you believe that man asked Paul how he could become a follower of Jesus, a God who could forgive a broken, depraved sinner like him?

Despite what he had suffered, he wanted to return to the city where his wife and daughter were martyred for their faith. He prayed that he could one day preach the gospel there.

Would you believe that Paul was able to lead that man to faith in Christ and he became a Christian?

And would you believe that today that man is not only a deacon in that same church but leads their deacons and ministers to the people in that small congregation?

When Stephen was stoned to death, the killers laid their coats at the feet of a man named Saul, who gave approval to his death. This was the Jewish custom of "casting the first stone." The one who accused the other of blasphemy would throw the first rock if they were found guilty, then he would step aside and let the crowd finish the death sentence. It's in that small detail found in Acts 7:58 that we see Saul (later called Paul) as the one responsible for the killing of Stephen.

But the same Jesus whom Saul was trying to stamp out would soon come to him face-to-face, and that encounter with Christ would change everything.

On the hunt to arrest and kill more Christians, Saul was traveling to Damascus when he encountered Jesus on the road. Jesus called him by his name, knocked him to the ground, and told him it was a waste of time to fight against the kingdom of God. He should join it! And he did. Paul was reborn, and I believe it was largely because he'd seen how Stephen died.

The persecutor became a preacher.

The killer became a Christian.

The Pharisee came to faith.

This man would become known as Paul the apostle. He would write a large portion of our New Testament, plant churches around the Mediterranean, take the gospel into Rome, and become the single most powerful and influential force in all of church history as well as Western civilization. All because he watched a young Christian named Stephen die, and that testimony would haunt him until he met the Messiah and became the very type of person he had once tried to destroy.

Reborn for Eternity

Just like Paul from Acts, Paul from India was a persecutor of Christians until he met the very Christ he had been fighting against. Just like Paul from Acts, he paid a high price for following Jesus.

Today Paul is in the final season of his life as he struggles to eat, swallow, or even use the bathroom as a result of the physical damage done to his body by that angry mob decades ago. And yet, he believes that the moment he closes his eyes in death, he will open them in the presence of Jesus whom he encountered one day on the streets of India. He will see his wife and his daughter and every other martyr who laid down their life for the sake of the good news of God's love. But most importantly, he will see Jesus, radiant and shining with glory.

I met Paul over twenty years ago on my first trip to India. My encounter with him, as I heard the story of what he had suffered and lost for Christ, changed everything about my calling, my preaching, and the direction of my life.

When Jesus changes your life in this world, he also changes it in the next one. Eternity doesn't begin when you die. It's happening now. We are eternal beings made in the image of an eternal God, and we will all live forever, somewhere.

One glimpse of Jesus, one split second in his presence, and we'll know that everything we faced was worth it. When Jesus changes everything, it starts with our hearts, and our hearts go with us into eternity, forever changed and reborn.

TWELVE
How Jesus Brings Joy

There's a story in John's Gospel that illuminates our vision of Jesus because it gives us a glimpse of his views of women, extravagant generosity, and value of worship. If you've ever had questions about the way God feels about money, possessions, or people who give with ridiculous generosity, then Jesus's encounter with Mary immediately after the resurrection of Lazarus will be eye opening.

The surprise is an interaction between Jesus and a woman who steals the show by doing something for Jesus no one had ever done before. Matthew, Mark, and John all tell the story.

The Buzz about Jesus

When Jesus raised Lazarus from the dead, he let the cat out of the bag, so to speak. He could no longer fly under the rad Too many people saw it happen, and they all talked at which meant that the religious establishment sn? action with a plan to get rid of Jesus. He was to to the system they'd created.

"If we let him go on like this," they claimed, "everyone will believe in him, and then the Romans will come and take away both our temple and our nation." They went looking for him. His followers were also looking for him.

And while everyone was trying to find him, Jesus prioritized a party. He joined his friends in a familiar spot: Bethany.

Back in Bethany Again

A dinner was being held in Jesus's honor at the house of Simon the Leper to thank him for the gift he had just given to Mary, Martha, and Lazarus. They prepared a meal for their king. Though Jesus knew that the Jewish elite were on the warpath and would soon end his life, he chose to treasure the little time he had left on earth. Less than a week before his march to Golgotha, Jesus relaxed with food and friends.

True to their personalities, Mary, Martha, and Lazarus were relishing their time with Jesus in their own unique ways.

Martha, ever the gracious hostess, showed her undying gratitude by serving him and the rest of the dinner guests.

Lazarus was soaking it all in, reclining at the table with Jesus and delighting in his presence. After the recent turn of events, he would have taken on a new appreciation for the re acts of eating, drinking, and laughing.

the dinner guests reclined around the table after the vould have been a familiar setting: all men. The with hed and served. The men ate and talked.

shoulders, made a surprise entrance. She came forward f gratitude, her hair hanging loosely at her ong and flowing.

In that culture, women wore their hair up with their heads covered when they were in public or in mixed company. A woman would only let her hair down in her home, with her husband or her closest family. Added to that, she was holding a small and incredibly valuable container that surprised all of the dinner guests.

In Mary's hands was a pint of pure nard, a rare and expensive imported perfume. What Mary held was the equivalent of a year's wages. Let that sink in. To purchase such a bottle of perfume would have cost Mary a sizeable portion, if not every penny, of her savings. In plain English, that bottle of perfume was worth $40,000 to $50,000.

Where did she get this valuable commodity? Most likely it was passed down to her from her family, possibly her father, as a dowry gift that she would have taken into her marriage. The fact that she still had it meant that she wasn't married. Was she too old to marry now? Was there something about her past that made her undesirable as a wife? We don't know. But we do know she held her entire life savings, her very future, in her hands as she brought the gift to Jesus.

A woman crashed the men's party. With her hair down. Holding fifty grand in her hands. Everyone was watching her, but the only person she was watching was Jesus.

A woman crashed the men's party. With her hair down. Holding fifty grand in her hands. Everyone was watching her, but the only person she was watching was Jesus.

She discovered a powerful truth: nothing we give to Jesus is wasted. There is no amount too great, no sacrifice too costly, and no treasure on earth that can compare to having intimacy with

Christ. When Jesus comes to visit our house, we can't let him leave without an extravagant gift. If Jesus has come into our life and made our heart his home, it is only natural to fall at his feet in awe and worship him.

A Priceless Gift

So, whether she bought the nard with her hard-earned money or it was given to her for her wedding day as a dowry gift to offer her husband's family, it was valuable.

As everyone watched, she began to pour it over Jesus, using her own hair to wipe his feet with it. Mark 14 tells us that she broke the jar, cracking the seal that would have guaranteed its costly value, and poured it on his head. Matthew 26 tells us that it was an alabaster box commonly used to contain such precious nard, and she poured it on his head as he reclined on the ground at the table.

John, who saw the whole thing, recalls the story by saying she poured it on his feet and then washed his feet with her hair, adding that "the house was filled with the fragrance of the perfume" (John 12:3). Obviously, she broke the seal on the protective alabaster box, then took out the inner jar. She started at his head and poured the perfume on his body, ending at his feet, symbolically taking the position a slave or a servant would take to wash the feet of dinner guests with a towel. Except Mary used her hair, not a towel.

In explaining the cultural importance of a woman's hair, Paul wrote in 1 Corinthians 11:15, "If a woman has long hair, it is her glory . . . her hair is given to her as a covering" (CSB). Mary is laying her glory at the feet of Jesus.

In a moment of unrestrained adoration, Mary poured her heart and soul into worshiping Jesus.

Every element of Mary's posture was significant, and there's much we can learn from watching how she interacted with Jesus.

She could have easily given Jesus the opulent gift in dramatic fashion, on a platter with a big shiny bow. She could have boasted about the cost of the perfume, telling Jesus and the dinner guests how, wanting to be selfless, she had liquidated her bank account to buy him an outrageously expensive gift. Or that she gave him her dowry. That certainly would have painted Mary in a pious light.

But there was no need for words. Her posture spoke for her. In line with the tradition of anointing kings, Mary poured the regal perfume upon Jesus from head to toe.

Decorum went out the door. She wasn't concerned that his stinky, mud-caked feet might dirty her clean hair. There were rags in the kitchen and cloths in the closet that could have been used, but Mary chose to lower herself before him, abandoning any concern for her appearance.

Her presence in the room and her over-the-top display didn't go over well with all of the dinner guests, and neither will your full devotion to Jesus always be celebrated by the people around you.

As fate would have it, it was Judas Iscariot who spoke out against Mary's actions. "Why wasn't this perfume sold and the money given to the poor?" he objected (John 12:5). "It was worth a year's wages," he continued, as if Jesus and the rest of the table were unaware of the cost of the perfume.

While Mary's focus was locked intently on Jesus, Judas could only see dollar signs. Judas acted like he cared for the poor, but he only cared about his pockets. John tells us that Judas's consternation had nothing to do with feeding and clothing the needy. Judas responded the way he did "because he was a thief; as keeper of the money bag, he used to help himself to what was put into it" (v. 6). John had probably watched him do it, more than once, as they traveled together with Jesus for almost four years.

Whatever the reasons, the root of Judas's contempt for Mary's actions was a heart issue. Judas couldn't see the big picture, blinded to the beauty in Mary's sacrifice. He couldn't fathom what her gift or posture truly meant. The type of worship Mary exhibited was foreign to his hardened heart.

But what man saw as foolish, Jesus saw as beautiful. Worship seldom makes sense to a world that's results-oriented and focused on the bottom line.

Judas, offended that a woman would dare enter the men's space, rebuked her publicly in a home where he was a guest, before all of her friends and family. In other words, things were getting awkward.

How would Jesus respond to how Judas just spoke to Mary?

As he does so often, Jesus surprised everyone.

Turning to face Judas, Jesus said, "Leave her alone" (v. 7).

Even the shyest of the dinner guests probably looked up from the table in shock. Judas was one of Jesus's twelve disciples, and a trusted one at that. He kept the money bag, yet Jesus rebuked him, coming to the defense of the woman who chose to worship.

Jesus always knows our motives. He sees what we do, but more importantly, he knows why we do it. He doesn't refuse gifts we bring to him, big or small. The value of what we give to Jesus is not tied to how much we paid for it, or even how much money we give to our church or a ministry. The value is attached to our motivation. When we give because we love, Jesus accepts and calls it worship.

Leave Her Alone

Jesus knew Mary. He knew the sacrifice and gratitude that coalesced in her act of worship, and he received it regardless of whether or not it made sense to anyone else.

The symbolism of Mary's actions went even deeper than reflecting her devotion. After telling Judas to leave Mary alone, Jesus explained the significance of her sacrifice. "It was intended that she should save this perfume for the day of my burial. You will always have the poor among you, but you will not always have me" (vv. 7–8).

Jesus always knows our motives. He sees what we do, but more importantly, he knows why we do it.

Jesus made it clear that Mary was doing more than just lavishing a worshipful gift upon her king. She was anointing him, preparing him for his death, which was imminent. Once again, Jesus foreshadowed what was awaiting him in Jerusalem, but this time it was different. There was a heightened sense of urgency to his words that suggested his final hour had arrived.

Kings were anointed with oil in the Old Testament at their inauguration to a position of power. Dead bodies were also anointed, wrapped in cloth, and covered in oils and spices upon their death. Here, in the house of Simon the Leper, Mary honored Jesus as King of Kings, but he was a different king altogether. He would rule and reign, but not until he died and was raised from the grave. The nard she poured on his body was a kingly anointing, signifying his death as a sacrifice and his resurrection as power over the greatest enemy of humanity: death itself.

He had spelled it out plainly. Mary would have plenty of opportunities to serve the poor. They weren't going anywhere, but Jesus was.

Jesus knew what awaited him in Jerusalem. Perhaps Mary did too. He had, after all, just resurrected her brother. Mary had a crucial role to play in the final week of Jesus's time on earth, preparing him for what lay ahead on the cross.

Be like Mary. Break the unspoken rules if you have to. Defy the expectations of others and get as close to Jesus as you can. Worship him. Talk to him. Tell him everything that's in your heart, and even what's in your head. Be emotional about it. Laugh and shout and weep; lift your hands and sing at the top of your lungs. When you have to choose between keeping the status quo or embarrassing yourself for Jesus, throw dignity out the door and dive on your face before the King of Kings.

Everything that Jesus ever did and all that he does now is so that we will believe in him. He wants us to trust him, to put our full faith in him, to give him total control of our lives. He wants to save us from our sins, from our shame, and from ourselves, and he'll go to any lengths to do it. The salvation that starts when we first ask Jesus to come into our life continues; it goes on and on until we are physically with Jesus in eternity.

Get Extravagant

Have you ever done something extravagant for Jesus? We don't have him sitting in our home and we can't pour perfume on his head and feet, so for us, doing something extravagant for Jesus most likely means doing it for another person.

Mary's love for Jesus literally overflowed everywhere. The more you love Jesus, the more that love will overflow onto others.

Have you ever considered inviting someone to live in that spare bedroom in your home? Do you have an extra car that you could honestly live without? What if you gave it to a single mom or a struggling college student, or even to a man who just got out of prison and needs help getting back on his feet?

Do you know a family in your neighborhood or at your church that can barely pay their bills because of a medical emergency? What if you paid one of their bills this month: their electricity bill, their grocery bill, or even their house payment? Could you afford to pay for a student's summer mission trip? Would you offer to volunteer as a chaperone on that mission trip, or as a leader for your church's summer camp for students?

Do you have a dinner table and food in your kitchen? Why not invite some people over to sit at that table and eat food with you, and while you're at it, consider asking someone completely different from you, from a different ethnic background, or an immigrant family from another country, just to show the love of Jesus and get to know someone you'd usually overlook?

The point is to give extravagantly because you have received extravagant grace. We deserve judgment and punishment but we receive mercy and love. It shouldn't be too hard to give like we have received.

What Mary gave Jesus that day was much more than a thank-you gift for bringing her brother back from the dead.

It was an example for us to follow. Jesus loves it when we're generous. He won't refuse our gift. He won't criticize it. He'll receive it, especially when we give it to someone else in his name.

Jesus chose to honor an unconventional, awkward display of worship. He defended a woman kneeling at his feet, tears streaming down her face and dirt and oil caked in her hair. He silenced the one who questioned her to draw attention to her lavish love and extravagant worship.

The feet she wiped would be nailed to a cross in a matter of days. The place she put her hair would one day bear the scars of a crucifixion and resurrection.

He knows you and he loves you. When you come to him and worship without concern for tradition or expectations, he won't dismiss or shame you. You can bless Jesus with the gifts you bring him, so bring them often.

Africa and the Egg

I lived in Africa as a short-term missionary in college. I stayed with a family who lived in the bush of Kenya. I slept in their modest home on top of a wool blanket. I spent my days traveling on foot from village to village, preaching in small churches and under big trees by the side of the road and visiting families in their homes. I prayed for the sick and shared the gospel in every home as my interpreter, Isaac, taught me about his culture and his people and their customs.

Each village had a cluster of thatched-roof huts made of mud, straw, and sticks usually surrounding a well in the middle, with fifty to sixty residents. Most of them had never seen a white person before, but they'd heard of America and immediately showed great hospitality when Isaac told them I was a minister from the United States.

They worked every day of their lives just to survive. Most had never owned a pair of shoes, and none had running water or indoor toilets. Yet the thing I remember most about the beautiful Kenyans was their unbridled and immediate generosity.

Sickness and physical deformities were commonplace. They had no access to doctors, hospitals, or medicine. Many died prematurely of treatable sicknesses or infections. The family I lived with had eight children, with only five of them surviving past childbirth.

I wanted to take each of them home with me to get them the medical attention that we take for granted, but since that was not an option, I simply embraced each of them with handshakes and hugs, picked up every child in my arms and kissed their forehead, laid hands on every man and woman to pray for blessing and healing, and ate whatever sparse food they could spare to honor me as a guest when I entered their villages.

In one such village, Isaac walked me into the home of a very sick old woman. No one knew what was wrong with her, only that she was frail and dying. She lived alone, having survived her husband. Her children tried to care for her, but poverty affected every family, so there were days she didn't have a single bite of food. If she did eat, it was the result of charity from other villagers, usually in the form of leftover ugali (an African cornmeal mush), cassava, or boiled eggs. She was skin and bones.

As we ducked to enter her one-room mud hut, I saw her sitting on a mat on the floor with both her legs, atrophied and lifeless, tucked underneath her. She was blind. The only items in her home were a small wicker basket, a metal bucket, a stool, and a towel.

When Isaac announced our arrival, she began to stir, pulling her body across the floor with one hand, holding her other hand out toward me, as if asking me to take it. I did. Then with my hand firmly inside hers, she slid over to the wall and plunged her other hand into the tiny handmade wicker basket. She dug under the towel that was inside it and pulled back something clutched in her fist, as if it was some small treasure she'd been saving for a special occasion.

She opened her hand to reveal one single egg. She then opened up my hand and gently put the egg in my palm, then closed my fingers around it with hers and patted the back of my clutched fist as a smile grew across her weathered face, underneath her blind eyes.

I heard Isaac moaning beside me, and as I glanced his way, tears were cascading off of his chin and landing on the dirt floor. He knew this woman. He knew she was dying. We had walked many miles that day in hopes that we could see her and pray for her before she died. He told me that egg was the only food she would have that day, and possibly for many days to come, if she lived that long.

How could I take the only food she would have, possibly the last food she would ever taste, before she passed into eternity?

When I attempted to give it back, Isaac said, "Oh no, brother, you must not give it back. She is honoring you as a man of God. She will be more blessed if you take it than if she eats it. She has never had a guest like you visit her, a sick old woman who is dying. Please, now, pray for her."

As I knelt by her mat and placed my hand on her shoulder, I could feel the sharp bones beneath her skin. She asked me to preach the good news of Jesus to her again, informing me that she was a Christian and she was going to heaven soon, but that to hear the gospel from an American in her own home would be the greatest joy for her before she died. I finished my prayer and she sang a song in Swahili about the goodness of God and the sacrifice of Jesus.

As Isaac and I walked back to my house that evening, the sun descended behind the acacia trees, the air grew cool, and the sounds of Africa at dusk became a symphony of nature joined in a chorus of worship. I clutched that hard-boiled egg in my hand the whole way back. I was too afraid it would break if I put it in my pack. I wondered if I could get it back to America without breaking it so that I could somehow have it preserved. I wanted to keep it forever.

Isaac asked me, "Brother, don't you like eggs? You should eat it. It will turn rotten if you don't."

I said, "Oh, yes, I like eggs. But this one is special."

I still remember that small egg as one of the most precious gifts anyone has ever given me. It cost that woman almost everything to give me what she had, and the value of that gift was tied to the motive of her heart. She sacrificed. It was small. And it was sacred.

My encounter with her was an encounter with Jesus. She taught me about sacrifice, hospitality, generosity, and true kindness. Sharie and I make financial decisions now, almost thirty years later, influenced by that crippled and blind woman who saw Jesus more clearly than I ever had.

When we're reborn, Jesus changes our affections. He becomes the object of our love and worship. In turn, we gladly lay down anything we have for the sake of blessing Jesus and others. This is the fruit of the reborn life.

A Different Kind of Math

Whether it's falling on your face at an altar, giving an insane amount of money to a ministry near to your heart, or having a come-to-Jesus moment in your car as worship music plays at a red light, he sees your heart.

You don't need an alabaster box of perfume. You can give an egg. We serve a God with a different economy. He uses a different kind of math.

A widow gives two pennies in the offering and it's more than the richest Pharisee ever gave.

We serve a God with a different economy. He uses a different kind of math.

One lost sheep gets more attention and energy than ninety-nine sheep safe in the pen.

A day laborer who works one hour gets paid just as much as the ones who worked all day long.

The least and the last are called the greatest and the best.

The only relevant opinion belongs to the God who didn't hold back his passionate display of love for us on the cross. So go for it. Give big. Hold nothing back. Lose your cool, embarrass yourself, break the rules, and worship!

THIRTEEN

How Jesus Restores Relationships

By now we know that being reborn is more than a prayer you pray or a cute religious concept. It is salvation, and it encompasses everything about you. Jesus does more than forgive you of your sins. That's just the start. He changes everything.

He redeems your past regrets. He restores broken relationships. He reminds you of your true identity. He rescues you from wasting your life chasing money and fame. He gives you a seat at the family table. He places you in a community called the church. He defends you. He dignifies you. He transforms your affections. He breaks addictions. He gives you patience in persecution and endurance in suffering. He heals you, calls you by your name, and becomes your friend.

And he prepares a place for you in heaven, giving you the assurance that you will live forever with him and his people.

These stories from the New Testament are about real people who met Jesus and were saved, changed, and reborn. We can see ourselves in these stories. We can also think of people we know who have similar life stories. They need to be saved, made new, reborn. We can point them to Jesus. We have to, because we love them.

I wanted to leave you with one more story of how Jesus changes people, even a witch who hadn't spoken to his mother in thirty-seven years.

When I was on the way to my truck one Sunday night after preaching, an excited woman approached me in the parking lot. She was visibly filled with energy, and it manifested itself in a smile that stretched from one ear to the other.

"Clayton, I have to tell you this story. I hope you have a minute because I just can't wait." She was in luck. I love people. I love stories. And I love happy, excited people with stories.

I stood there, mouth open and bug-eyed, while she explained how her dad, a witch in the Wiccan religion, was reborn just days before he died.

"My dad was around church people his entire life. He lost a lot. His mom left him after a nasty divorce when he was only two. He experienced abuse. He went to church sporadically, but usually because of a girl. His first wife of twelve years with two children died in a car accident. 'Church people' told him things like 'She deserved it,' 'It was for the best,' 'You must've done something terrible for God to punish you this way,' and 'You're better off without her.' At thirty-four years old, he walked away from Christianity and started studying Hinduism, Buddhism, and finally the Wiccan religion. When I left home he was a practicing witch. He believed in God, just not the one named 'Jesus' that those cold-hearted, hateful Christians claimed to follow.

"I became a believer at sixteen and started praying for my dad's salvation. As the years passed, I tried to show Jesus to my dad, but he refused to believe. He said my belief in Christ was no more significant than the Wiccan belief in Mother Earth, and that by being a good person and sending out 'light' that we can be part of the 'good' in the universe.

"By 2015 I'd been praying for my dad to be saved for twenty years. Any time I would get a chance to share the gospel, something would always interrupt us. It was disheartening. Through my small group's encouragement, I fasted and prayed for weeks that God would do 'whatever it takes' to save my dad. I heard a little voice whisper 'lung cancer.' I prayed 'Give me the grace to handle it, but whatever it takes, please save him.'

"In October 2016 my dad coughed up blood for the first time. He lived four hours away, so my husband and I brought my parents into our home so that we could care for them.

"Two months later we learned that my dad had lung cancer. He was told that he had a year to live and that the treatment would kill him faster than the cancer. He opted to fight it with natural medicines, and if they didn't work, he was better off dying from the cancer than the treatment.

"The whole time my dad had been in our home, my small group from church had been asking to come meet him and pray with him. They kept sending food and doing whatever we needed help with. Dad got to see firsthand what true followers of Christ are like. My friends would drop by to hang out with him, look at his guitars, or just talk to him. One sweet friend even brought Christmas gifts—one for each night in December for each person in our family!

"Dad was so blown away by the outpouring of genuine love that he couldn't help but notice something was 'different' about me and my friends from 'that church.' At the risk of sounding boastful (I'm not!) my dad saw me give up so much of my life and time just to care for him that he would tell me very frequently how much he appreciated what I was doing and that he couldn't repay me. I would always answer, 'It's not me, it's Jesus.'

"On Friday night, January 13, 2017, twelve of our friends arranged a dinner at a Mexican restaurant for the specific reason of meeting my father and praying for him. After we ate, my friend Susan asked my dad if he wanted to pray to receive Christ. He said no, and honestly, I was heartbroken. After we got home I had a heart-to-heart with God. I reminded him that he promised if I ask anything according to his will that he would answer me. I reminded him that I was doing my part to show my dad what a true believer looked like, and that I was sacrificing everything so my dad would be saved. I got angry because it seemed like God had totally ignored our prayers.

"Moments later, while I was washing dishes, my dad came in and just stood beside me. Then he said words that are etched onto my heart forever. 'I see something in you and your friends from that church that I have never seen before. There is a light, peace, and love in all of you. How did you get that?'

"I looked at my sweet seventy-four-year-old daddy and said, 'Yes, we have a personal relationship with the Creator of the universe. In him is light, and in that light, there is no darkness. His name is Jesus.' His next question brought me to my knees. 'How do I get to know him? Your Jesus isn't the Jesus that I've ever known. I want to know him.' I sat down and read Scripture from Romans with my dad, and then I held his hand as he prayed to receive Christ at 10:33 that night!

"There is no greater joy in this world than that. I have led all three of my children to Christ—but that was something different—something supernatural.

"His health declined, and on May 16, 2017, my dad said he saw angels in his room, and that made him smile and want to leave this world. On May 18 he closed his eyes on earth and opened them in heaven.

"But there's more.

"Three weeks before my dad died, the Lord put it on my heart to try to reach his mother. Because of her doing, they had been estranged for thirty-seven years. I had no contact info. In a strange way, I sensed the Lord put the name 'Susan' on my heart, and I did a Facebook search. The first 'Susan' to pop up was a name I'd vaguely remembered my dad mentioning. I contacted her and my message went something to the effect of 'This is awkward and random, but I think we're related; my dad is dying; if you can contact his mom and let her know, I'd appreciate it. Just thought she should know.'

"Well, this 'Susan' wasn't random after all. It was her! His mom! Within five minutes of me sending the message, she and I were on the phone. She had been praying for a way to contact my dad when I felt the Lord speaking to me to find her!

"Would you believe that my grandmother (his estranged mother) had just received Christ as well and had been looking to get in touch with my dad? She had no idea he was sick. She simply wanted to be reunited with him.

"The very next day, my dad heard his mother's voice for the first time in thirty-seven years. As soon as he said hello, she started saying, 'I love you, I miss you, I'm so sorry!'

"Two days later, my ninety-three-year-old grandmother came from Birmingham just to be able to hug her son for the

"My ninety-three-year-old grandmother came from Birmingham just to be able to hug her son for the first time in thirty-seven years." first time in thirty-seven years. Before she left, she told him that she was so glad they both had been born again so they could be together in heaven and she could spend eternity making up for the wrong she had done to him on earth. They were reconciled three weeks before he died. How good is Jesus?"

>>>>>

If you have felt something happen in your heart while you've been reading *Reborn*, maybe that's the Holy Spirit inviting you to be . . . reborn! If so, I want to tell you how to take your first step of faith into a new relationship with Jesus.

Like the two men who walked with Jesus to Emmaus, all you have to do is invite him into your heart, and he will say yes. It begins with a simple, honest prayer. Not a religious ritual, but a humble conversation where you ask Jesus to save you.

You can talk to him right now, right where you are. He's listening.

Jesus, I've felt you move in my heart, and I want to know you. Please come into my life right now. I invite you in. Would you save me from my sin and make me a new person from the inside out? I repent of my sin and receive your love. I give you my heart and my life. I want to follow you and be your disciple. I love you, Jesus. Thank you for saving me! Amen.

Acknowledgments

Thanks to the authors, pastors, professors, and scholars who have inspired and educated me on the person of Jesus and the culture in which he lived: N. T. Wright, F. F. Bruce, Will Durant, John Stott, Tim Keller, Joachim Jeremias, Elyse Fitzpatrick, Eugene Peterson, Beth Moore, Ray Vanderlaan, Robby Gallaty, Brad Young, Bruce Metzger, Abraham Heschel, Craig Keener, D. A. Carson, and Rodney Stark.

To Arie Bar David, perhaps the sharpest mind and the deepest well of knowledge, wisdom, and understanding of the Jewish roots of our Christian faith alive today.

To my friends and brothers for their partnership in life and the gospel: Justin Brock, Brad Cooper, Jordan Hibbard, Brian Burgess, Dan Lian, Todd Gaston, Daniel Lucas, Josh Gardner, Greg Wells, Lee McDerment, Tim McKnight, James Noble, Bruce Frank, Derwin Gray, J. D. Greear, Bruce Ashford, Shane Duffey, and Tracy Jessup.

To Evans Whitaker for your unparalleled depth of kindness and wisdom.

To Regi Campbell for your love and investment into so many men, including me.

To Parker King for your insights, hard work, and invaluable assistance.

CLAYTON KING is founder and president of Crossroads Missions and Summer Camps and Clayton King Ministries, teaching pastor at NewSpring Church, and distinguished professor of evangelism at Anderson University. The author of seventeen books, including *Stronger* and *Overcome*, King regularly speaks to hundreds of thousands of people all over the globe. He and his wife, Sharie, are winners of the Young Adult Book of the Year Award from the Christian Retailer's Association for *True Love Project*. They have two sons and live in South Carolina. For more information, visit www.claytonking.com.

Steps to Peace With God

1. God's Purpose: Peace and Life

God loves you and wants you to experience peace and life—abundant and eternal.

The Bible says ...

"We have peace with God through our Lord Jesus Christ." *Romans 5:1, NKJV*

"For God so loved the world that He gave His only begotten Son, that whoever believes in Him should not perish but have everlasting life." *John 3:16, NKJV*

"I have come that they may have life, and that they may have it more abundantly." *John 10:10, NKJV*

Since God planned for us to have peace and the abundant life right now, why are most people not having this experience?

2. Our Problem: Separation From God

God created us in His own image to have an abundant life. He did not make us as robots to automatically love and obey Him, but gave us a will and a freedom of choice.

We chose to disobey God and go our own willful way. We still make this choice today. This results in separation from God.

The Bible says ...

"For all have sinned and fall short of the glory of God." *Romans 3:23, NKJV*

"For the wages of sin is death, but the gift of God is eternal life in Christ Jesus our Lord." *Romans 6:23, NKJV*

Our choice results in separation from God.

Our Attempts

Through the ages, individuals have tried in many ways to bridge this gap ... without success ...

The Bible says ...

"There is a way that seems right to a man, but its end is the way of death."
Proverbs 14:12, NKJV

"But your iniquities have separated you from your God; and your sins have hidden His face from you, so that He will not hear."
Isaiah 59:2, NKJV

There is only one remedy for this problem of separation.

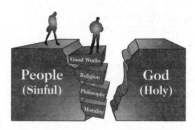

3. God's Remedy: The Cross

Jesus Christ is the only answer to this problem. He died on the cross and rose from the grave, paying the penalty for our sin and bridging the gap between God and people.

The Bible says ...

"For there is one God and one Mediator between God and men, the Man Christ Jesus."
1 Timothy 2:5, NKJV

"For Christ also suffered once for sins, the just for the unjust, that He might bring us to God."
1 Peter 3:18, NKJV

"But God shows his love for us in that while we were still sinners, Christ died for us." *Romans 5:8, ESV*

God has provided the only way ... we must make the choice ...

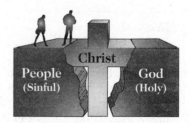

4. OUR RESPONSE: RECEIVE CHRIST

We must trust Jesus Christ and receive Him by personal invitation.

THE BIBLE SAYS ...

"Behold, I stand at the door and knock. If anyone hears My voice and opens the door, I will come in to him and dine with him, and he with Me." *Revelation 3:20, NKJV*

"But to all who did receive him, who believed in his name, he gave the right to become children of God." *John 1:12, ESV*

"If you confess with your mouth that Jesus is Lord and believe in your heart that God raised him from the dead, you will be saved." *Romans 10:9, ESV*

Are you here ... or here?

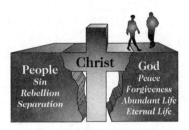

Is there any good reason why you cannot receive Jesus Christ right now?

HOW TO RECEIVE CHRIST:

1. Admit your need (say, "I am a sinner").
2. Be willing to turn from your sins (repent) and ask for God's forgiveness.
3. Believe that Jesus Christ died for you on the cross and rose from the grave.
4. Through prayer, invite Jesus Christ to come in and control your life through the Holy Spirit (receive Jesus as Lord and Savior).

WHAT TO PRAY:

Dear God,

I know that I am a sinner. I want to turn from my sins, and I ask for Your forgiveness. I believe that Jesus Christ is Your Son. I believe He died for my sins and that You raised Him to life. I want Him to come into my heart and to take control of my life. I want to trust Jesus as my Savior and follow Him as my Lord from this day forward.

In Jesus' Name, amen.

_____   _____
Date   Signature

God's Assurance: His Word

If you prayed this prayer,

the Bible says ...

"For 'everyone who calls on the name of the Lord will be saved.'"
Romans 10:13, ESV

Did you sincerely ask Jesus Christ to come into your life?
Where is He right now? What has He given you?

"For by grace you have been saved through faith. And this is not your
own doing; it is the gift of God, not a result of works, so that no one may
boast." *Ephesians 2:8–9, ESV*

the Bible says ...

"He who has the Son has life; he who does not have the Son of God does
not have life. These things I have written to you who believe in the name of
the Son of God, that you may know that you have eternal life, and that you
may continue to believe in the name of the Son of God."
1 John 5:12–13, NKJV

Receiving Christ, we are born into God's family through the
supernatural work of the Holy Spirit, who indwells every believer.
This is called regeneration or the "new birth."

This is just the beginning of a wonderful new life in Christ. To deepen
this relationship you should:

1. Read your Bible every day to know Christ better.
2. Talk to God in prayer every day.
3. Tell others about Christ.
4. Worship, fellowship, and serve with other Christians in a church where
   Christ is preached.
5. As Christ's representative in a needy world, demonstrate your new life by
   your love and concern for others.

God bless you as you do.

Franklin Graham

If you want further help in the decision you have made, write to:
Billy Graham Evangelistic Association
1 Billy Graham Parkway, Charlotte, NC 28201-0001

1-877-2GRAHAM (1-877-247-2426)
BillyGraham.org/commitment